The Executive Guide
to Operational Planning

George L. Morrisey

Patrick J. Below

Betty L. Acomb

The Executive Guide
to Operational Planning

Jossey-Bass Publishers · San Francisco

THE EXECUTIVE GUIDE TO OPERATIONAL PLANNING
by George L. Morrisey, Patrick J. Below, and Betty L. Acomb

Copyright © 1987 by: Jossey-Bass Inc., Publishers
350 Sansome Street
San Francisco, California 94104

George L. Morrisey
Patrick J. Below
Betty L. Acomb

Library of Congress Cataloging-in-Publication Data

Morrisey, George L.
  The executive guide to operational planning.

  (The Jossey-Bass management series)
  Bibliography: p.
  Includes index.
  1. Corporate planning.   2. Strategic planning.
I. Below, Patrick J. II. Acomb, Betty L. III. Title.
IV. Series.
HD30.28.M65   1987   658.4'012   87-45508
ISBN 1-55542-064-8 (alk. paper)

Manufactured in the United States of America

The paper used in this book meets the State
of California requirements for recycled paper
(50 percent recycled waste, including 10 percent
post-consumer waste), which are the strictest guidelines
for recycled paper currently in use in the United States.

JACKET DESIGN BY WILLI BAUM

FIRST EDITION
   HB Printing   10 9 8 7 6

Code 8747

The Jossey-Bass

Management Series

Contents

What Is an Operational Plan? • Why Do You Need an Operational Plan? • What Is the Integrated Planning Process? • How Does the Operational Plan Fit into the Integrated Planning Process? • What Are the Elements of an Operational Plan, and How Do They Fit Together? • What Is the Most Effective Approach to Developing an Operational Plan? • What Are the Benefits of This Operational Planning Process? • In Summary

What Are the Benefits of Involvement and Commitment? • What Are Some Obstacles to Gaining Ongoing Involvement? • What Can Top Management Do to Get More Involvement and Com-

More Effective? • How Is the Total Organization's Budget Determined? • How Are Resources
Allocated Through the Budgeting Process? •
How Does Control Fit into the Budgeting Process? • In Summary

What Are the Benefits of Unit Operational
Planning to Middle and First Line Managers? •
When and How Are Unit Operational Plans
Developed? • How Does Top Management Know
When There Is an Effective Unit Operational
Planning Process in Place? • In Summary •
Supplement: Developing Unit Roles and Mis-
sions • Why Should There Be a Statement of
Roles and Missions for Each Separate Unit? •
Where Does That Statement Come From? • How
Should Unit Statements Be Prepared? • Key
Questions for Evaluating Unit Roles and Mis-
sions • What Are Some Examples of Unit Roles
and Missions? • In Summary

Where Are You with Operational Planning? •
What Is Involved in Implementing an
Organization-Wide Approach? • What Does an
Operational Plan Look Like? • When May
Strategic and Operational Planning Be Com-
pleted Together? • What Is Different About
Planning in Public Sector Organizations? •
What Is the Difference Between an Operational
Plan and a Business Plan? • What About Man-
agement by Objectives? • What About Follow-
Up? • In Summary

Figures

Preface

Operational planning is coming of age. Executives and managers at all levels are searching for practical ways to improve their performance through more effective management and planning processes. In order to meet today's challenges, on both an individual and an organizational basis, it is imperative that operational planning be effectively practiced cross-functionally. Operational planning is the implementation arm of strategic planning. While strategic planning helps the CEO and the executive team create the vision and direction for the future, it is only through operational planning that this vision and direction comes alive.

This book is specifically designed to help executives and managers develop and implement realistic, results-oriented plans that will meet *both* the long-term and short-term needs of their organizations. Critical questions this book addresses include:

- What is the most practical process for getting executives and managers throughout the organization involved in operational planning?
- How are operational plans best developed from a total organization perspective?

- What must be done to ensure that operational plans are implemented at all levels in the organization?

Operational plans traditionally have been developed along functional or departmental lines. The logic behind this is that most organizations are managed by function (for example, marketing, engineering, sales, manufacturing, and finance). Thus, operational plans are developed, by and large, by individuals and teams with a strong functional orientation. However, executives are now realizing that operational planning needs to be done on an integrated basis across functional lines in order to address complex organizational performance issues such as total quality, improved productivity and profitability, and development of a strong customer orientation.

For this to happen, top management's role, including that of the CEO, must be to structure the operational planning process to make sure that this integration takes place throughout the organization. Operational plans must contain projected accomplishments that cross functional or departmental lines. In addition, measurement systems must be devised to ensure that these results are being achieved.

Many organizations perceive the preparation of a budget as their primary means of operational planning. However, operational planning is far more than budgeting; it projects and describes the specific results and actions required for the organization to be successful, both short term and long term. In fact, effective operational planning makes the budgeting process more realistic by integrating budgets with the operational plans. A major purpose of this book is to define and develop operational planning as a management tool for achieving *total* organization results and to establish the premise that planning must be an ongoing managerial function, not merely an annual event.

For Whom Is This Book Written and How Can It Be Used?

Operational planning, as described in this book, is best done on an organization-wide basis. Therefore, this book is written for the entire management team, from the CEO and senior executives to first line managers and key employees. Organizations interested in developing and expanding their operational planning process to include their entire management team can use this book as a practical guide to ensure that everyone is on a common wavelength regarding operational planning philosophy, concepts, and terminology.

In addition to organization-wide application of operational planning, this book also has particular value for the following:

1. *CEO/COO and the executive team*—for determining their particular roles in the operational planning process
2. *Department heads or other middle managers*—for developing their own operational plans in support of the total organization
3. *First line managers and other key employees*—for developing and implementing unit operational plans
4. *External or internal consultants*—for guiding management teams in the development, integration, and implementation of operational plans
5. *Management seminar or class instructors*—as a primary, supplementary, or reference text for classes in operational planning or management
6. *Prospective managers*—in preparing for future responsibilities

An executive/management team with a strong philosophy and commitment to involving their people in planning can make this operational planning process work for them. In the final analysis, people, not plans, produce results. And a planning process that is well organized and consistently applied is an effective management tool to assist in the achievement of those results.

Why Was This Book Written?

This book was written to clarify and simplify the discipline and practice of operational planning. There are, of course, numerous books on planning. However, planning books, like planning in general, frequently present confusing terminology and concepts. As a result, it is unclear to many managers exactly how to go about instituting, or upgrading, their planning process. Despite the high degree of management interest, many books on planning have not really clarified and simplified the process in such a way that it addresses many of the issues that organizations are facing.

It is our conviction that planning, as a discipline, needs to be better defined and organized in order for it to be applied at all levels within an organization. We have been using the planning process described in this book for many years with our clients. A common benefit that these clients have shared with us, following their use of the process, is that now *all* their managers really understand planning and have both a common terminology and a framework within which to develop and communicate their plans. Our intent in this book is to share that benefit more broadly: to contribute to making operational planning a better defined, better understood, and, as a result, better practiced discipline.

This book is also designed to provide a direct tie-in with strategic planning and results management—something no other book that we are aware of does. While this book stands alone as a clear guide to the whys and hows of operational planning, it is designed as a part of a three-book series on what we refer to as the "Integrated Planning Process." The first book in the series, *The Executive Guide to Strategic Planning,* shows how to determine the concept and direction of the organization for the future. The third book will delineate the process of results management, which ensures the execution of both the strategic and operational plans.

Overview of the Contents

The chapters in this book flow in accordance with the normal development of an operational plan. Chapter One discusses what operational planning is, its place in the

Integrated Planning Process, and the definitions of each of the six elements of an operational plan with an explanation of how they fit together. Chapter Two is concerned with getting total organizational involvement in and commitment to the operational planning process. It describes some of the factors that keep people from becoming more committed and what top management can do to encourage greater involvement and commitment. It also defines specifically the key roles of individual managers in operational planning.

The next two chapters cover the elements managers must go through prior to the determination of specific objectives. Chapter Three describes how to develop an operational analysis, a frequently overlooked step in the operational planning process. It includes a step-by-step process for completing an operational analysis that can be adapted to any organization. It also serves to identify issues requiring cross-functional integration. Chapter Four combines two elements, key results areas and indicators of performance. Since these are frequently developed at the same time, it is appropriate to examine them together. This chapter focuses on determination of the specific areas that require identifiable results and the measurable factors that will be used to describe those results.

Chapter Five gets into the formulation of specific operational objectives. It also describes the relationship between objectives and standards of performance and provides guidelines for writing clear-cut objectives. Chapter Six covers the process of preparing detailed action plans, including provision for horizontal integration among functional units.

Chapter Seven shows how to integrate budgets with the operational plan. This is not a detailed description of how to prepare an organizational budget; there are several excellent books already available on this process (see the Annotated Bibliography). Rather, it addresses the process of determining, allocating, and controlling an organization's resources, while achieving the results identified in the earlier elements of the operational plan.

Chapter Eight describes how to make the operational planning process come alive at the departmental and unit levels. While the basic operational planning process is essentially the same for an individual unit as for the total organization (with a considerably narrower focus), there are some distinctions; these are addressed in this chapter. In addition, there is a chapter supplement that shows how to develop a statement of unit roles and missions (for those organizations that do not have provision for such a statement).

Chapter Nine provides a practical summary of operational plan development and implementation from start to finish. It includes a method for assessing your current planning processes to determine what areas need improvement as well as specifics on setting up an effective plan development process. It includes references to such things as application in the public sector and relationship to a business plan and to management by objectives. An Annotated Bibliography describing some of the other works in the field that have influenced the development of this book is included at the end.

How Did This Book and Series Come About?

As indicated earlier, this book on operational planning is book two of a three-book series on the Integrated Planning Process. The Integrated Planning Process is outlined in Chapter One. This management framework was initially developed by Patrick Below in his domestic and international consulting work. The operational planning component is based largely on George Morrisey's contributions to the field of management. In 1983, Below and Morrisey joined with Betty Acomb to develop plans to document the entire planning process. The result is this three-book series on planning.

Our collaborative efforts also fostered the formation of a national network of planning consultants and trainers called the Planning Process Group. A major purpose of this group is to advance both the state of the art and the ongoing practice of planning in organizations of all sizes.

Since the publication of the first book in this series, it has come to our attention that readers may want to contact us to offer feedback on the process we have described or to delve deeper into it with us. In the interest of facilitating such efforts, we can be contacted as follows: George L. Morrisey, P.O. Box 5879, Buena Park, California 90622 (phone 714/995-1244), and Patrick J. Below and Betty L. Acomb, Patrick J. Below Associates, Ltd., 1000 West College Avenue, Appleton, Wisconsin 54914 (phone 414/733-3500).

Acknowledgments

Many people have contributed their ideas and concepts to the development of this book. Our thanks go to the many executives and managers in client organizations we have served, in both the private and public sectors, for their feedback in the refinement and improvement of the planning process described in this book. The members of the Planning Process Group have also contributed ideas as a result of applying these planning concepts with their individual clients.

We are particularly grateful to Marie J. Kane (a business planning consultant and a charter member of the Planning Process Group) for her many good ideas and thoughtful review of our initial manuscript. We are also indebted to three practicing executives who reviewed the manuscript and made many worthwhile suggestions: John Bagby, Jerry Connelly, and Roy Serpa.

In addition, there have been several individuals along the way who have influenced our thinking and approach to the planning process. In particular, we would like to thank George Odiorne for his many contributions both to the practice of management and, through his personal support and encouragement, to this three-book series. Donn Coffee, a long-time colleague of George Morrisey's, provided exceptionally useful feedback on this manuscript, in addition to his contributions to the original development of many of these concepts.

Our thanks also go to Tim Rinker and Joseph Ferrell for their contributions to the graphic designs and illustrations in this book, and to Betty Stubbs for her always cheerful attitude and outstanding work in typing (and retyping) our manuscript into a final product.

September 1987   George L. Morrisey
                                   Buena Park, California
                                   Patrick J. Below
                                   Appleton, Wisconsin
                                   Betty L. Acomb
                                   Appleton, Wisconsin

The Authors

George L. Morrisey is chairman of the Morrisey Group, a management consulting firm based in Buena Park, California, and a principal in the Planning Process Group, a nationwide network of independent planning consultants. He received his B.S. (1951) and M.Ed. (1952) degrees from Springfield College in Massachusetts. Morrisey has more than twenty years' experience as a practicing manager and key specialist with such organizations as First Western Bank, Rockwell International, McDonnell Douglas, and the U.S. Postal Service, in addition to more than fifteen years as a full-time speaker, trainer, and consultant. He has personally assisted more than 200 business, industrial, service, governmental, and not-for-profit organizations in the areas of strategic and operational planning.

Morrisey is the author, or coauthor, of fourteen books, including *The Executive Guide to Strategic Planning, Management by Objectives and Results for Business and Industry, Management by Objectives and Results in the Public Sector, Performance Appraisals for Business and Industry, Performance Appraisals in the Public Sector, Effective Business and Technical Presentations,* and *Getting Your Act Together: Goal Setting for Fun, Health, and Profit* (which complements the popular Salenger Educational Media film with the same title, which features Morrisey and for which he served as adviser). He is the author and producer of several audio- and videocassette learning programs, all directed toward helping individuals and organizations become more effective and self-fulfilled.

Morrisey received the Council of Peers Award for Excellence (CPAE), the highest recognition granted to a professional speaker, from the National Speakers Association in 1984 and the national American Society for Training and Development (ASTD) Award for Publications in 1974. He is a member of the boards of directors of the Association for Management Excellence and the National Speakers Association and is on the Advisory Board for the Society for the Advancement of Management's (SAM) *Advanced Management Journal.*

Patrick J. Below is president of Patrick J. Below Associates, Ltd., a management consulting firm in Appleton, Wisconsin, founded in 1970. His firm specializes in working with small and medium-sized companies in the design and implementation of the Integrated Planning Process (strategic and operational planning). He received a B.S. degree (1962) in electrical engineering from Marquette University and an M.B.A. degree (1967) from Indiana University in Bloomington, Indiana.

Below's work experience includes management-level positions with the General Electric Company and the American Can Company from 1962 through 1970. Altogether, he has twenty-five years of business management experience in the areas of manufacturing management, sales and marketing, computer systems design, human resource development, and business planning. Below's broad-based background, coupled with his seventeen years' experience as an international business consultant, has uniquely qualified him to serve as an effective planning coach/facilitator in leading senior executive teams in developing, or upgrading, their planning process.

Below is a member of Beta Gamma Sigma, an honorary business administration fraternity, and of the Institute of Management Consultants (IMC) and is a Certified Management Consultant (CMC). He is also a member of the College of Managing Consultants and is the lead author of *The Executive Guide to Strategic Planning*.

Betty L. Acomb is a senior partner in Patrick J. Below Associates, Ltd., a management consulting firm in Appleton, Wisconsin, specializing in strategic and operational planning. She is also one of the three principals in the Planning Process Group, a nationwide network of planning consultants. Acomb received her B.A. degree (1973) from Buena Vista College in Iowa and has undertaken postgraduate studies at the University of Wisconsin at Madison.

Acomb has ten years' experience in public sector management in the areas of strategic and operational planning, program management, community development, and legislative programming. She has served as director of the Community Contact Program (Cincinnati, Ohio) and program manager of Community Action (Rock County, Wisconsin). In addition, she is a member of the Institute of Management Consultants (IMC) and is a Certified Management Consultant (CMC). She is coauthor of *The Executive Guide to Strategic Planning*.

The Executive Guide
to Operational Planning

What Is Operational Planning?

In the classic movie *Ben Hur*, the most exciting scene is a marvelous chariot race with Charlton Heston and his team of horses racing around the track at breakneck speed to eventual victory. Imagine what would have happened if, during that race, one or more of the horses had suddenly veered to the right or stopped altogether.

Many organizations resemble a chariot being pulled by a team of horses. The various segments of the organization, such as marketing, production, and finance, have to pull together if that organization is to win its own race. An effective operational plan, and planning process, is like a set of reins in the hands of a skilled chariot driver that allow the horses to reach optimum performance with clear and firm guidance toward the desired result.

Operational planning clearly defines what an organization intends to accomplish, how and when this will take place, and who will be held accountable. It is also the means by which an organization's strategic plan is implemented. The operational planning process starts with the senior executive team's determination of short-term results required to carry out the organization's mission and strategy. While the strategic plan is primarily the arena of upper management, every manager and key employee within the organization must understand the operational plan and determine the specific results for which he or she will be held accountable.

1

This requires each major organizational unit to have its own operational plan in support of that of the total organization. Furthermore, these plans must be linked, horizontally as well as vertically, with those of other interfacing units. This linkage comes as a result of an integrated, organization-wide operational planning process, which is the focus of this book.

Agreement must be reached on the following for an operational planning process to be effective:

- *Terminology.* The exact meaning and interpretation of the terms used must be consistently understood and applied by all who must make the plan come alive. Within this book, these terms are described in clear, explicit language that leads to this consistency. Incidentally, some organizations use terms such as *business plan, short-term plan,* or *profit plan* to refer to what we are calling the *operational plan.* Terms other than those in this book that are in common usage in specific organizations may be substituted as appropriate, provided they are used consistently.
- *Simplicity.* Operational planning must not be seen by people within the organization as a cumbersome, complicated process. While a significant amount of effort is required, the process itself, as illustrated in this book, is quite simple and straightforward.
- *Approach.* There needs to be complete understanding and agreement on the operational planning approach to be followed. While there are various ways to develop and implement an operational plan, the approach described here is clear and precise, with ample opportunity for adapting it to any organization's needs.
- *Extent of involvement.* Operational planning needs to be addressed at all managerial levels and, at some point, may involve most, if not all, key employees. While the planned results to be achieved by the total organization are the responsibility of top management, middle and first line management play major roles in making sure those plans are implemented.

- *Separation of operational from strategic planning.* These are two distinctly different thinking and planning processes. Strategic planning requires visionary and directional thinking and normally is completed early in the fiscal year. Operational planning requires short-term, specific thinking and typically is completed during the latter part of the fiscal year in preparation for the next year's efforts. Under certain circumstances, however, it may be desirable to have an operational plan without a strategic plan. For example, an organization faced with a short-term crisis, such as inadequate cash flow, may develop an operational plan designed to resolve that crisis without regard to a strategic plan. A strategic plan, on the other hand, is unlikely to have much impact without a supporting operational plan to serve as an implementation vehicle.

What Is an Operational Plan?

There are two separate considerations in operational planning—the plan and the process. An operational plan is a document identifying specific results to be achieved within a given time period (usually one year). It also includes the specific actions and resources required to accomplish these results. Six distinct elements make up this plan.

- Operational analysis
- Key results areas
- Indicators of performance
- Operational objectives
- Action plans
- Budgets

Together these six elements form an important management tool for determining specific short-term results to be achieved and fixing accountability for those results.

The operational planning process is the ongoing involvement of operating executives, managers, and key employees in producing operational plans for the total organization as well as for their individual organizational units. A particular strength of this process is its emphasis on team planning through a series of well-organized meetings. It is this aspect of the process that builds organization-wide belief in, and commitment to, the operational plan, because it gives the participants ownership. It is this same commitment that helps to ensure implementation of the plan.

Why Do You Need an Operational Plan?

Have you ever been on a trip, reasonably sure you knew where you were going, and ended up getting lost because you missed a key turn or failed to anticipate a potential detour? Even though an organization has a good track record of success and skilled leaders at the helm, an effective operational plan, which is the equivalent of an up-to-date road map, is needed to make sure that desired results are actually achieved. It is an integral part of the management of any organization. As such, its purpose is:

- *To achieve short-term operating results.* These include, but are not limited to, such areas as financial results, sales performance, new product development, new markets/ customers, and people development. These results tend to be more specific and detailed than those identified in the strategic plan.
- *To implement the current year's portion of the organization's strategic plan.* The operational plan is the primary means by which the strategic plan is carried out; thus the operational plan and the strategic plan must be carefully integrated.
- *To ensure that all parts of the organization are pulling together.* This is really where the concept of the Integrated Planning Process becomes crucial. Since most objectives for the total organization require active input from various departments or units within the organization, there must be a clear and united focus on the results to be achieved.

Furthermore, organizational unit plans, when addressing specific organizational issues, must not be in conflict with plans of other units. Cross-functional review and integration of unit plans is an important step in building organizational teamwork.

- *To involve, and get commitment of, all key people in meeting organizational objectives.* The operational plan is dependent on the contributions of key people at all levels throughout the organization. The planning process serves as a communications vehicle for this involvement. In order to feel a sense of commitment to the total organization's plan, people must see where they fit into the plan and how they can make a significant contribution to it. The operational plan should be widely distributed and discussed to ensure understanding and commitment. It should be viewed as a document accessible to everyone in the organization.

In many cases, it may appear that portions of an operational plan belabor the obvious. Yet how often has the "obvious" been the one thing that has been overlooked! For example, a company is ready to launch a major sales campaign only to discover that new catalogs won't be ready for another six weeks. Or a new product or service is being introduced, but no provision has been made for training related personnel. The operational planning process represents both a discipline and a communications vehicle. It is as necessary to the success of any organization as its people, financial resources, products, and technology. No viable organization can continue to succeed and grow without a clearly defined operational plan. It is at the heart of what we refer to as the Integrated Planning Process.

What Is the Integrated Planning Process?

The Integrated Planning Process, as developed by Patrick Below, represents a total view of an organization's planning and control system. Figure 1.1 depicts the three

Figure 1.1. Integrated Planning Process.

major components—Strategic Plan, Operational Plan, and Results Management.

All three components are necessary to achieve consistent organizational results. However, each of the three components serves a distinctly different purpose. The strategic plan focuses on the basic concept (mission) and direction (strategy) of the organization. The operational plan concentrates on how to implement the strategic plan and produce short-term results. The results management component is concerned with comparing performance with plan (both strategic and operational) and ensuring the achievement of results. Thus, although each component serves a different purpose, they are highly integrated; no part of the planning process can be effectively carried out in isolation. In order to make operational planning work in an organization, these three components of planning, and how they fit together, need to be clearly identified.

The principal elements that make up each component are outlined in Figure 1.2. The purpose of this graphic is to provide the CEO (chief executive officer or key decision maker) and the senior executive team with a visual portrayal of the total planning process. This diagram can serve as an excellent communications tool for providing a similar picture throughout the organization.

Figure 1.2. Integrated Planning Process Elements.

Strategic planning, which is covered in the first book of this series, *The Executive Guide to Strategic Planning,* is, by its very nature, broad-based and conceptual. The strategic plan addresses the long-term critical issues facing the organization in the future. It also deals with the future in terms of strategy, long-term objectives, and integrated programs for accomplishing those objectives.

Primary responsibility for developing or updating the strategic plan rests with the CEO and the senior executive team. This effort is usually undertaken early in the fiscal year. This allows ample time for completion of the strategic plan prior to development of the organization's operational plan. This is important, because they are two completely different planning processes and content of the operational plan is likely to be directly influenced by decisions arrived at during development of the strategic plan.

Many organizations attempt to do strategic and operational planning at the same time. This is rarely, if ever, successful. When both strategic and operational issues are discussed, the urgency of operational issues tends to dominate. Strategic planning requires considerable external analysis and broad-gauged thinking by the CEO and the executive team. Operational planning, in contrast, tends to be more internally oriented, is specific and detailed, and requires the investment of considerable time and effort by middle and first line management. The focus of the strategic plan is concept and direction. The focus of the operational plan is implementation and results.

The operational plan, the middle component, plays a different role than does the strategic plan in the organization's planning process. Whereas the focus of strategic planning is on what business the organization should be in and what direction it should be going in, the operational plan focuses on the organization's short-term destination and how it is going to get there. Typically, the time frame for the operational plan is one year, and it is generally developed during the latter part of the prior fiscal year. The operational plan needs to be developed *after* the strategic plan (which is usually prepared early in the year), since one purpose of the operational plan is to implement a portion of the strategic plan.

The third component, *results management,* closes the loop on the total planning process. It provides management with an ongoing mechanism for executing and monitoring the implementation and results of *both* the strategic and operational plans. The first two components address the development of plans; results management is primarily concerned with plan execution. Activities that take place here are ongoing, unlike those of the strategic and operational plans, which are developed during specific periods of the year. To make planning a continuous, dynamic process within an organization, particular attention and emphasis must be given to results management.

The CEO needs to be the chief architect of the Integrated Planning Process. This includes the integration of all three components: the strategic plan, the operational plan, and results management. While logic suggests that the process start with the development of a strategic plan, management may choose to begin with any one of the three components where a particular organizational need is evident. Another important ingredient in the process is the active involvement and commitment of the people within the organization. As the people who need to make the organization more successful become better informed about, and more actively involved in, the various planning steps, their commitment to significant results will become increasingly substantial. Remember, the purpose of planning is not to produce plans; it is to produce results. Planning is a people process and the focus in this book is on making it work at all levels.

How Does the Operational Plan Fit into the Integrated Planning Process?

The operational plan, as shown in the Integrated Planning Process diagram (Figure 1.2), is at the center of the process. As the implementation arm of the strategic plan, it serves as the bridge between broad-based vision and specific, ongoing results.

The primary role of the operational plan is to identify the short-term results and actions needed to carry out the organization's long-term mission and strategy and to meet current organizational needs. Many organizations tend to put most of their planning effort into the development and implementation of their operational plans. While it is possible to move directly into operational planning without a clear strategic focus, it will be more effective if a strategic foundation is established first. The operational plan should also be totally integrated with the results management component to ensure that desired results are achieved by analyzing and monitoring performance in relation to that plan. Truly successful organizations recognize the need for addressing the *entire* process.

Figure 1.3. Operational Plan Framework.

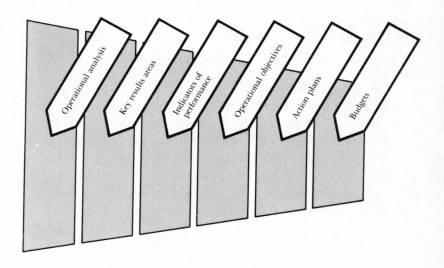

What Are the Elements of an Operational Plan, and How Do They Fit Together?

The operational plan is made up of six primary elements, shown in Figure 1.3. This is a slight adaptation from the MOR funnel that George Morrisey introduced in his various publications on Management by Objectives and Results (see the Annotated Bibliography). However, in this case, the emphasis is on organizational, rather than individual, application.

The funnel graphic illustrates the fact that managerial planning and decision making move from the broad and general to the narrow and specific. Part of the job of management in developing the operational plan is to reduce the size of managerial decisions by breaking them down into smaller pieces. The process starts with a relatively broad element and gets narrower and more specific as it moves on down the line.

If the organization preparing its operational plan has already developed a strategic plan, the first order of business, of course, is to review that strategic plan. This is to ensure that there is a clear understanding of the concept and direction of the organization and that critical issues are addressed. It is especially important to be familiar with the organization's statement of mission before starting to develop an operational plan. If there is no strategic plan to refer to, then development of a statement of mission for the organization might be a part of the operational analysis step in the process. This may include a requirement for identifying organizational unit roles and missions where unit plans are required. (See the supplement to Chapter Eight for instruction on developing an organizational unit statement of roles and missions, which can also be adapted for use with the entire organization.)

1. *Operational analysis.* This is an assessment of the current status of the organization's performance and of the specific issues that will have substantial impact on the business during the coming year. These are identified from:
    *   A review of the strategic plan for factors requiring short-term attention—for example, the need for a market analysis as a prerequisite to developing a new product line
    *   A review of the prior year's operational plan and performance for issues that will carry over into the plan year—for example, expansion of a newly introduced service
    *   Pinpointing other issues or current problems likely to impact operations for the plan year—for example, an anticipated technological breakthrough
2. *Key results areas.* These represent those priority areas within which *results* need to be achieved during the projected operational planning period. While operational analysis draws attention to critical issues or problems, the use of key results areas ensures continuity in important performance areas that may not represent problems but are, nonetheless, essential to organization results. At the total organizational level, these are likely to include categories related to such areas as financial

results, sales performance, and new product development. Normally, these will be broad enough to include results from more than one department or organizational segment. At the unit level (*unit* includes any distinct entity within the total organization, from a division or department to a one-person operation), key results areas focus on the principal outputs of that particular unit, which could include such things as quality improvement, productivity, cost control, and employee morale.

3. *Indicators of performance.* These identify those measurable factors within each key results area on which specific objectives may be set. Since there are many ways in which results can be measured, it is important that management clearly identify and agree on those indicators that will provide the *best visibility* on desired results. Consequently, indicators also serve as factors that can be tracked by managers monitoring progress toward objectives. Indicators that can be quantified, such as units or dollars of sales, units of production, and percentage of market share, are very useful and usually easy to track. However, other indicators that are not as easily quantified, such as program implementation, research and development capability, and new product introduction, are also valuable in assessing the type of results desired. In any case, the indicators selected must be understood and agreed to by those involved.

4. *Operational objectives.* These represent the specific, measurable results to be accomplished within the time span of the operational plan. They derive from the key results areas and incorporate indicators of performance as the principal measurable factors in the objectives themselves. Objectives at the total organizational level normally require effort across unit lines and contain either a specific target date or an implied fiscal-year completion. They are limited to the major organizational accomplishments projected for the period of the operational plan. At the unit level, objectives tend to be narrower and more precise. For example, an organizational objective to

generate a minimum of 10 percent of sales from new products may require specific unit objectives by product and by region at lower levels. These operational objectives need to be either directly in support of the long-term objectives in the strategic plan (if one exists) or compatible with them. For specific results that are continuous in nature and may not require detailed action plans, such as minimum gross margin or monthly production quotas, the use of standards of performance, rather than objectives, may be more useful. A standard of performance represents a level of achievement to be reached and maintained on an ongoing basis.

5. *Action plans.* These represent the specific actions required to accomplish each of the operational objectives. They may be stated in one or a combination of the following three forms:

    • Specific activities or events that are not necessarily interrelated

    • A series of interconnected events following an analytical or problem-solving approach

    • A series of smaller or shorter-term objectives

    Action plans include specific time frames, resource requirements, and accountability. They also should include appropriate feedback mechanisms so that management can verify that the plan is being met.

6. *Budgets.* The primary purpose of a budget is to indicate the level of financial resources required for the organization to achieve its objectives. While budgets appear as the final element in the operational plan, they are an integral part of the process and, as such, they normally provide a financial structure for plan preparation. Operational planning, including the preparation of budgets, should be seen as an iterative process throughout, with information generated in one element directly influencing the content of another. For example, if budget preparation reveals the limited availability of certain resources, specific objectives or action plans may require modification.

What Is the Most Effective Approach
to Developing an Operational Plan?

The approach required for development of the organization's operational plan includes determining who should be involved and when and how they should be involved. The approach recommended is one that *integrates* top-down and bottom-up planning, taking advantage of the favorable aspects, while minimizing the unfavorable aspects, of each.

Top-down planning refers to organizational plans that are developed initially at the executive level and communicated downward for review, refinement, and additional input. Top-down planning may also refer to operational plans in major organizational segments, such as divisions, functional departments, or large geographical centers, developed in support of that of the total organization.

Bottom-up planning refers to the development of unit operational plans, following upper-management guidelines, that reflect unit issues and needs. These are submitted upward for review, modification, and consolidation into higher-level plans.

Integrated planning combines the two, resulting in plans that address both top-down and bottom-up needs. The process frequently starts with the identification of critical operational issues at the top level, which are then communicated downward prior to development of the total plan. The primary advantage to this approach is that there is a clear sense of direction for unit planning without the feeling that everything is predetermined, resulting in optimum creativity within the guidelines established. The primary disadvantage is that the process may take somewhat longer than a strictly top-down approach. Integrated planning results in the most productive approach to operational planning, provided there is a real sense of openness and flexibility on the part of both top management and unit leadership. Typically, members of the senior executive team can expect to spend anywhere from three to five days of group effort, in two or three separate meetings, putting together an operational plan for the total organization. Time invested at the unit level may be less than that, depending on the scope of results to be addressed.

What Are the Benefits of This Operational Planning Process?

Operational planning, as described in this book, has several distinct benefits:

1. It provides a clear and distinct linkage to all related elements in the strategic plan. This ensures that the operational plan is either directly connected to or compatible with the strategic plan. It also provides both vertical and horizontal linkage, where appropriate, with unit plans throughout the organization.
2. It provides a standard planning methodology that can be applied to the total organization and to each unit within that organization without introducing new terminology. This increases the likelihood that managers throughout the organization will be on the same wavelength.
3. It provides a simplified process that can be adapted easily to organizational requirements. This could include unique planning demands from a parent company or a superagency.
4. It follows a logical progression from broad areas of interest to narrower and more specific results and actions. This increases the likelihood that general issues will be translated into meaningful accomplishments.
5. It provides clear direction to individual managerial and key employee plans throughout the organization. This increases the likelihood that everyone will be pulling in the same direction.
6. It provides a sound basis for closing the loop through the results management component of the Integrated Planning Process. This ensures the accomplishment of desired results on a consistent basis.
7. It can also be used as a powerful team-building process at every organizational level. As managers and key em-

ployees meet together to discuss, analyze, and reach agreement on planned results and related actions, they are more likely to be supportive of each other in efforts to achieve those results.

In Summary

Operational planning is at the heart of what we refer to as the Integrated Planning Process. It provides a basis for implementing a portion of the strategic plan as well as for determining specific short-term results. An operational plan is a document identifying specific results to be achieved within a given time period (usually one year), together with identification of the specific actions and resources required to achieve these results. The operational planning process is the ongoing involvement of operating executives, managers, and key employees in producing operational plans for the total organization as well as for their individual organizational units.

The operational plan is made up of six primary elements: operational analysis, key results areas, indicators of performance, operational objectives, action plans, and budgets. The approach is distinctive in that it provides an important linkage to the rest of the Integrated Planning Process.

Operational planning requires the active involvement and commitment of all key people within the organization. This is accomplished through the development of unit operational plans and through the senior executive team's efforts in determining total organizational requirements. This involvement and commitment is essential to the effective implementation of these plans, as will be addressed more specifically in the next chapter.

2

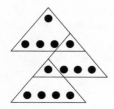

Ensuring Organization-Wide Involvement

"Having lost sight of our objectives, we redoubled our efforts!" This truism can be applied to the planning process just as much as to any other organizational effort. In your organization, does operational planning tend to be an eleventh-hour activity to meet a deadline? Is there more concern about the proper completion of forms than about clear identification of results to be achieved? Is operational planning treated as an annual event rather than an ongoing management process? Is planning perceived as a burden rather than a managerial priority? A yes to any of these questions reflects a need for more meaningful organization-wide involvement in the planning process.

Commitment, in this case, means that key people at all organizational levels, nonmanagerial as well as those with management responsibility, have an opportunity to understand and participate in the formulation of the operational plan at their own levels. This participation may include specific contributions during executive-level plan development, review of a draft version of the total organization's plan with an opportunity for comments and suggestions, and/or identification and submission of unit plans that support the total plan. In other words, those charged with the responsibility for achieving the results identified in the plan have a real sense of ownership of and commitment to both the plan and the planning process.

What Are the Benefits of Involvement and Commitment?

Operational planning requires the active involvement of all key people in the organization, from the CEO on down. To achieve this involvement, senior management must demonstrate, by both word and deed, their own commitment to the process. This means that senior executives must be personally involved and must encourage and reinforce the participation of others. This involvement and commitment will produce:

- *Consistent results.* There is a high correlation between individual involvement in and commitment to a plan and the achievement of consistent results. A plan that is developed by one person or group and handed to others for implementation may lead to *compliance*—they will carry it out as a condition of continued employment—but will rarely foster *commitment.* Compliance usually results in minimal performance—they will do what has to be done, but not much more; commitment tends to produce optimal performance. The potential payoff from people who are committed provides a tremendous return on investment compared to the cost of involvement.
- *More realistic plans.* When key people on the firing line are encouraged to make honest and realistic assessments of what is achievable, there is a much greater likelihood that realistic plans will be established and, more important, carried out successfully. The district sales manager, the applications engineer, and the customer services supervisor are likely to know what is really required to assure success in their areas of responsibility.
- *Improved communication and coordination.* Active involvement in the planning process leads to a clearer understanding, by all individuals, of what is expected of them and of others. This understanding facilitates communication across organizational lines through a common frame of reference—the plan. Furthermore, those who have a vested interest in achieving specific objectives quickly

realize the value of their planning efforts when they have the support of their counterparts in other parts of the organization. A natural conclusion is the recognition that the best way to get support from someone else is to identify and provide whatever support may be sought by the other party. This results in a win-win situation for everyone concerned.

- *Increased accountability.* The active involvement and commitment of all key employees in the development of the operational plan produces accountability for carrying out various portions of the plan. Furthermore, acceptance of this accountability is much higher among those employees who play a significant role in determining the content of the plan.

What Are Some Obstacles to Gaining Ongoing Involvement?

A decision by senior management to get the active involvement and commitment of all key people in the operational planning process does not guarantee that it will automatically happen. There are some built-in resistances in many people that may get in the way. Below are some typical reactions that suggest a less-than-wholehearted desire to become an active participant. Included are some possible explanations for these reactions and some ways they might be addressed.

"We've got too many meetings already." This is a common expression of frustration related to the time commitment required in operational planning. However, the frustration expressed here is not so much a resistance to meetings as it is to meetings that are perceived as nonproductive. Typically, people involved in operational planning efforts are busy, productive people who see meetings that drag on interminably as keeping them from other, more important duties.

Effective operational planning does require a commitment of time, part of which is spent in meetings for coordination and integration of plans to ensure that everyone is pulling in the same direction. Meetings that have clear expectations of what will be accomplished, to which participants come prepared, that move crisply, and that are completed on time are viewed much more positively.

"Planning is just another papermill." Paperwork is the bane of many operational planning efforts. Some people view planning as filling out forms and writing reports. While a certain amount of paperwork is both inevitable and necessary, it can and should be controlled. Morrisey's Law states that *the utility of any document is in inverse relationship to its length.* The most frequently used document is likely to be no longer than a single sheet of paper.

A major purpose of paperwork in the planning process is to provide a communications vehicle for establishing performance expectations and relating progress against those expectations. Keeping the paperwork under control by focusing on the critical few results required at each level is more likely to get the active involvement and commitment of those who have to make the plans work.

"Why bother? I can't control what other departments do." Many people in organizations feel frustrated when they perceive that they are held accountable for certain results, portions of which are the responsibility of other departments. For example, a marketing manager may need a detailed computerized report from data processing in order to complete a critical market analysis. The data processing manager, however, may have committed all available resources to a unit operational plan that does not include market analysis support. How often managers find that their number one priority ends up being number thirty-two on another person's list of thirty-one! Is it any wonder that such a situation leads to a feeling of helplessness and frustration?

While certain conflicts of this nature are inevitable, many of them can be avoided or minimized through the use of cross-functional team planning. In the above example, had the marketing manager involved data processing in the original development of the plan, there would be a greater likelihood of completing the market analysis on time.

What Can Top Management Do to Get
More Involvement and Commitment?

The senior executive team must set an example if the operational planning process is to be carried out effectively throughout the organization. Their actions must be considerably more direct and explicit here than in strategic planning, since far more people within the organization will be involved.

- *Visible commitment from above.* Senior executives must be seen clearly by the rest of the organization as willing and able to devote the time and effort necessary to make the operational plan for the total organization a reality. They must be perceived as managing, individually and collectively, in an effective, efficient, well-planned manner. This includes placing a high priority on the development of plans within all organizational units reporting to them. This must be reinforced even further through the review process, which will be covered in the third book of this series.
- *Clear and realistic performance expectations, including provision for changing circumstances and priorities.* These include expectations regarding the use of the planning process itself, as well as the specific results and actions to be included in the operational plan. While these expectations need to be clear and explicit, other managers throughout the organization must feel that they can influence the nature of these expectations.
- *Training/coaching in planning process methodology.* As indicated earlier, operational planning has a distinct technology and discipline. This may necessitate some initial skill training built around the planning process being used by the particular organization. This training can be provided during the actual planning cycle, so that managers are learning while doing. It can also be addressed in management training programs that include application of learned skills to actual organizational issues

or problems. In addition to whatever formal training is required, ongoing coaching in the methodology is needed as the planning cycle is followed. Without formal attention to the knowledge and skills required in operational planning, it is virtually inevitable that many managers will resist putting forth the amount of effort required for true commitment.

- *Integration with performance appraisal.* Objectives and the achievement of results need to be tied in to the organization's performance appraisal system. This will enable individuals to see a direct relationship between the operational plan and their own individual roles in, and performance to, the plan.

- *Recognition and reward (including individual and group incentives).* These should be provided for those who do an effective job of both the planning and performance to the plan. The achievement of significant results alone may not necessarily represent effective management. The achievement of significant results in relation to plans established does. For example, the doubling of sales revenues by a sales force might look spectacular on the bottom line. However, if plans have not been established in anticipation of those results, the organization may find itself in serious difficulty as it tries to meet those commitments without adequate production facilities. If we accept the fact that planning is an important part of any manager's job, then those who do an effective job of it must be recognized and rewarded accordingly.

What Are the Key Roles in Operational Planning?

The responsibility for the development and implementation of the total organization's operational plan lies with either the CEO (or whoever is designated as the organization's key decision maker) or the COO (chief operating officer), if there is one. The senior planning team also includes major department heads, one or two key staff advisers, and whoever will be guiding the operational planning process. In addition, there needs to be active involvement by managers and other key employees at all levels as they develop operational plans for their own units. Let's examine briefly each of these roles as it applies to the development of operational plans.

1. *The CEO and/or COO* has the ultimate responsibility for the results that need to come through the total organization's operational plan. Strong leadership must be seen from the executive office in order to ensure that the operational plan is properly developed and implemented. A major responsibility of that office is to ensure that the operational plan is integrated with, and supportive of, the strategic plan, and that *cross-functional planning* takes place. It is up to the executive office to make sure that the operational plan really addresses such cross-functional issues as profitability, new product development, organization-wide marketing capability, and people development. Another important role is to ensure that organization-wide participation in the operational planning process is taking place at all levels. The CEO, of course, continues to be accountable to the board of directors for both the completion and submission of the operational plan.

2. *Members of the senior executive team* function in dual roles. In their capacity as members of the senior executive team, they serve as an extension of the office of the CEO/COO in the development of the total organization's operational plan. It is important that ground rules be established ensuring that the members of the executive team, when they are working on the total organization's plan, are representing the interests of the entire organization, not primarily those of their own functional or program responsibilities. These ground rules could include a continual focus on overall organizational objectives and needs, including such areas as profits, markets, products, quality levels, and people-related issues. Their second role is to provide leadership in the

development and implementation of an operational plan within their areas of responsibility.

3. *The planning process facilitator* is responsible for a number of efforts that may be carried out by a planning coordinator, internal or external coach/facilitator, and/or internal planning staff. These duties and responsibilities are designed to ensure that the operational planning process proceeds effectively and efficiently. They may include such activities as:

- Designing or modifying the planning process
- Training/coaching managers involved in the planning process
- Facilitating planning meetings
- Establishing and monitoring the planning schedule
- Coordinating and handling logistics of planning meetings
- Documenting and distributing records of planning meetings as well as the operational plans themselves

4. *Middle managers* are responsible for the development, coordination, and implementation of operational plans for each of the units under their supervision and for ensuring that those unit plans are in support of the organization's plan. Each of the elements of the operational plan, as described in this book, needs to be developed within the unit framework. These various unit plans are pulled together to ensure horizontal as well as vertical coordination, reducing the likelihood of either duplication of effort or effort gap. In addition, middle managers are responsible for interpreting higher-level plans throughout the units under their supervision.

5. *First line managers,* including certain one-person operations, will also develop their own operational plans, following the process described in this book. One way of approaching this is through the application of the "unit president" concept. Regardless of level in the organization, each manager is considered to be president of a company—that is, of that part of the organization that he or she heads up. That person's immediate supervisor

represents the board of directors. The president's job is to determine, with the board, what results are essential and to manage their *company* in the most effective way to achieve those results.

How Does Team Building Take Place in the Planning Process?

For planning purposes, a team normally consists of a manager and his or her direct reports. Typically, planning teams are formulated as shown in Figure 2.1. This means that most managers will serve on two teams—one as a member and one as a leader. The purpose of each planning team is to serve as an extension of the team leader in developing and implementing that unit's operational plan.

While most planning teams reflect a vertical structure, project-oriented organizations may have teams, headed by a project manager, that include key people drawn from different disciplines, as shown in Figure 2.2. Even a vertical planning team may include people from other parts of the organization to get their inputs on certain plans.

The planning process is a natural vehicle for team building. By having those that are most affected participate in the planning decisions, organizations receive the dual benefit of more realistic and accurate input and greater sense of ownership by those who must carry out those decisions. This also leads to greater mutual support among team members as they recognize and accept the need for working together toward common objectives.

A key to successful team building in the planning process lies in the team leader's establishing an environment in which open, frank communication takes place. By focusing on the results the team needs to achieve, team members are able to perceive the bigger organizational picture and where they fit in, both as individuals and as a team within the larger organization. The sharing of differing points of view, as well as the creative energy that is stimulated through active interchange, frequently results in significantly better plans

Figure 2.1. Vertical Planning Teams.

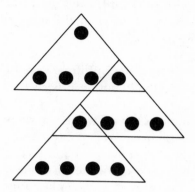

Figure 2.2. Horizontal or Cross-Functional Planning Teams.

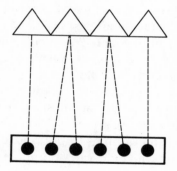

and better follow-through in carrying out these plans. This is a prime example of why the planning *process* may be more valuable than the plans developed.

In Summary

The effectiveness of an organization's operational plan and resulting performance to that plan is in direct proportion to the degree of involvement and commitment of the key people in the planning process. The benefits of involvement include consistent results, more realistic plans, improved communication and coordination, and increased accountability. There are a number of factors that may keep people from becoming more involved in the planning process. These include a feeling that there are already too many meetings and that planning is too much of a papermill. Furthermore, there is often a feeling of frustration because of the lack of support from other departments in accomplishing plans. The senior executive team must set an example in carrying out the operational planning process. This includes attention to the following factors: visible commitment to the planning process, clear and realistic performance expectations regarding plans and priorities, training/coaching in planning process methodology, integration of the operational plan with performance appraisal, and recognition and reward for those who do an effective job of operational planning and performance. The various operational planning roles of the CEO, COO, members of the senior executive team, planning process facilitator, middle managers, and first line managers need to be clearly defined so that the planning process can be carried out. An important aspect of operational planning is team building. This is enhanced by a planning process that promotes participation, open discussion, and mutual agreement and support at all levels within the organization. The ongoing involvement and commitment of all key people in the organization to both the plan and the process is the principal cohesive ingredient required in the development of an operational plan.

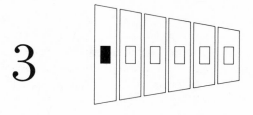

3

Developing an Operational Analysis

A frequent characteristic among results-oriented managers is impatience, which may lead to premature selection of objectives. There is often an intuitive feeling among managers that they already know what objectives should be set and what actions need to be taken to achieve results. While there is no question about the value of managerial intuition, it does not provide the total information base necessary for effective planning. Managers need to resist the natural temptation to jump immediately into setting objectives until they are *certain* objectives are being set on the *right* things. Therefore, it is no accident that the selection of objectives is the *fourth* element in operational planning rather than the first. Even if one or more managers have a clear perception of what is required, the planning team needs to go through some analytical effort prior to reaching agreement on objectives. Operational analysis helps the planning team identify and resolve the key issues. It increases the probability that objectives will produce the most productive and valuable accomplishments in the coming plan year. Operational analysis, the first element in the planning process, establishes an early focus for the plan.

What Is Operational Analysis?

Operational analysis is an executive-level assessment of the organization's performance and the major issues that will have substantial impact during the coming year. It provides the key link between the strategic plan and the development of the operational plan. It also examines short-term opportunities and threats, resource availability, and the major priorities that the planning team needs to establish for the coming year. The result of operational analysis is agreement by the planning team on specific conclusions and alternative courses of action on the most critical issues affecting organizational performance. This is not an in-depth analysis of organizational functions such as marketing, manufacturing, or finance. Rather, it is a broad-based analysis of issues that affect the total organization.

It is relatively easy to identify as many as twenty or thirty issues that need to be addressed by the organization. Operational analysis provides a basis for selection of the critical few issues that will make the greatest contribution to organizational results. It also ensures that there are no significant gaps between the strategic plan and operating requirements. Operational analysis:

- Establishes an information base from which realistic objectives and action plans are developed
- Ensures continuing focus on resolving the critical few issues throughout the planning process
- Integrates the long-term strategic needs of the organization with short-term operating requirements
- Provides understanding and agreement among the members of the planning team on the major issues facing the organization

A major advantage of using an issues-oriented approach to operational analysis is that people will see the relevance between the planning process and types of issues they are facing. Furthermore, this approach minimizes the amount of analysis required. By concentrating on issues, analysis is primarily limited to information that helps managers understand and address those specific issues.

Figure 3.1. Steps in Operational Analysis.

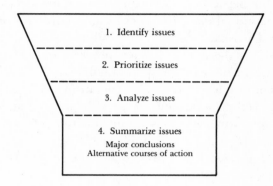

What Are the Steps in Operational Analysis?

There are four primary steps in conducting an operational analysis, as shown in Figure 3.1.

1. *Identify issues.* Develop a comprehensive list, from team members, of those issues likely to have significant impact on or contribute to operational performance in the coming year. These may be drawn from any or all of the following sources: the strategic plan (conceptual and long-term), the prior operational plan (specific and short-term), and actual performance (including current operating problems). Examples of these types of issues are:

Source	*Operational Issues*
Strategic plan	• Need for new product focus
	• Sources of future funding
	• Changing life-styles
Current operational plan	• Declining margins
	• Decrease in client population

Performance problems/   • Poor delivery
opportunities   performance
                             • Unanticipated increase in
                               demands for service

When a relatively large number of issues are identified, it
may be useful to group those that are related in order to
reduce overlap and to aid in the prioritization step.

2. *Prioritize issues.* Reach team agreement on the three to six
    most important operational issues—those that are likely
    to have the greatest impact on the total organization.
    Experience indicates that a limited number that truly
    represent the critical few issues stand a considerable
    higher chance of receiving the attention necessary to
    ensure effective resolution. Other issues deemed to be
    important may be delegated for action to a particular
    department or work unit or may be retained for periodic
    review and appropriate action in the future.

3. *Analyze issues.* Develop the supporting information
    necessary for team members to understand clearly the
    nature and scope of each critical issue. *Nature* addresses
    what appear to be the causes of an issue; *scope* addresses
    the likely size and impact of the issue on the organiza-
    tion's performance.

4. *Summarize issues.* Document the specific conclusions and
    alternative courses of action required to resolve the issues.
    These conclusions need to be supported by information
    generated in the preceding step.

How Is an Operational Analysis Produced?

Having identified the steps in the analysis process, we
offer some specific guidelines for completing each step. (An
example of a completed operational analysis is provided in
Figure 3.3, at the end of this chapter.)

1. *Identify issues.* A combination of the following techniques is an effective way to identify issues to be considered.

    a. A questionnaire may be completed individually by members of the planning team either in advance of or during the first part of the initial planning meeting. During the meeting, individual responses to these questions are shared and consolidated into a list of organizational issues, including both problems and opportunities. Questions such as the following may be included:

        • What are the two to three most critical issues facing the organization in the coming year? What is the probable impact that each of these issues will have on the organization?

        • What issues are likely to have the greatest effect on profitability (or short-term results) for the organization in the coming year?

        • What issues are likely to make the greatest contribution to the long-term success of the organization?

        • What changes have taken place or are likely to take place during the coming year that will significantly affect the organization's performance?

        • What specific cross-functional problems or opportunities are likely to have a significant impact on organizational performance?

        • What budget constraints are likely to affect organizational performance in the coming year?

    b. Group brainstorming is another effective technique for identifying critical operational issues. Since members of the planning team are frequently aware of these issues, this technique can generate a large quantity of ideas in a relatively short period of time. This technique can also be used to supplement the responses to the questionnaire.

    c. Existing strategic and operational plans, including performance to these plans, should be reviewed to

identify any additional factors that need to be incorporated into the issues list.

d.   Any critical performance problem areas not previously identified, such as severe quality problems or
major personnel shortages, also should be reviewed.

e.   Other sources of relevant information, such as
industry trends or demographic changes, may provide insight into issues that should be included.

After all potential issues are identified, they need to
be clarified and modified to make certain they are
understood by the team. Furthermore, issues that are
externally focused may need to be restated in terms of
their internal implications. For example, "international
monetary fluctuations" could be stated as "insufficient
safeguards to offset impact of international monetary
fluctuations." "Election year impact" (in a government
agency) might be addressed as "diversion of resources to
campaign-related issues." "Decrease in client population" would provide more direction when stated as "excess service capacity for declining client population."

When a relatively large number of issues are identified, it may be useful to group those that are related in
order to reduce overlap. For example, declining margins,
competitive price pressures, and increased raw material
costs might be addressed as a single issue, such as "need
for improved margins." The intent is to reduce the
number of issues to a manageable size—no more than ten
to fifteen.

2.   *Prioritize issues.* Having now clarified and modified the
potential issues and reduced them to a manageable number, the team should next agree on the three to six most
important issues for the organization to address during the
coming year. When necessary, these issues should be further
described in terms that have total organization significance.
For example, "impact of declining margins" could be
stated in terms of its dollar or percentage effect on profitability or in terms of the core product line affected.

A simple, but effective, technique for prioritizing is:

a. Have each individual team member identify his or her top three priorities using a 3-2-1 weighting factor, 3 being the most important.

b. On a chart, record the weighting factors identified by each individual team member alongside each issue.

c. Compile priorities based on both the number of responses and the weighted average.

d. Discuss the issues to ensure team agreement on priorities.

Issues not included in the final list should be referred to specific departments or work units, retained for later consideration, or eliminated.

3. *Analyze issues.* Once agreement has been reached on the most important issues, the next action is to develop and present supporting information on each issue. Two effective methods for this step are group discussion and individual assignments to be presented at a subsequent meeting. For each priority issue, there must be team consensus on responses to questions such as the following:

- What is the issue?
- What data/information is available (or needed) to resolve this issue?
- What appear to be the factors causing this to be an issue for the organization?
- What types of results are needed in this area?

4. *Summarize issues.* Having identified, prioritized, and analyzed the issues, the team now summarizes these into conclusions and alternative courses of action to be considered.

In the following example (Figure 3.2), the issue of excess service capacity for declining client population resulted in these findings:

Figure 3.2. Sample Critical Issue Analysis.

Issue:
- Excess service capacity for declining client population (from a community service agency).

Data/information:
- Actual client population has declined at an average rate of X percent a year for the past three years. Revised forecast shows that this will continue for at least the next three years.
- Average cost per client service has increased from X to Y over the past three years.
- Funding is based on a cost per client service. The established standard for next year's funding will be exceeded based on current projections.

Causes:
- Capacity has been developed to handle a certain forecast level of clients.
- Client population has declined owing to changing demographics.

Results needed:
- Average cost per client service must not be increased.
- Use of current capacity needs to be optimized.
- All current personnel should be retained, if possible.

Conclusions:
- Client population has been declining at an annual rate of X percent for the past three years and is being projected at the same rate for the next three years.
- Additional uses for service capacity need to be established or the cost of maintaining that capacity needs to be reduced.

Alternative courses of action:
- New sources of potential clients
- Additional services for current clients
- Subcontracting to other, similar organizations
- Retraining of current service personnel to other duties
- Downgrading or terminating selected personnel
- Closing/consolidating selected offices

In another example, an operational issue related to market share encroachment by a particular competitor led to these findings:

Conclusion:
- A substantial portion of market share loss has been to competitor X and needs to be regained.

Alternative courses of action:
- Improved customer research
- Upgraded product line
- Sales incentives

What Is an Example of Operational Analysis?

Figure 3.3, an example of a completed operational analysis, was adapted from the operational plan of a $30 million manufacturing company. It is intended for illustration only, so some of the detail from the actual plan has been deleted. In particular, the operational issues shown under the first step are those that came as a result of grouping and consolidating the issues identified in initial brainstorming.

In Summary

Operational analysis is the first element in the development of an operational plan. It is the step that ensures integration with existing strategic and operational plans by identifying, prioritizing, analyzing, and summarizing critical operational issues. As a result of this analysis, the planning team must agree on key conclusions for resolving the most important issues. The analysis may also lead to important inputs for departmental and other organizational unit plans. Operational analysis is an important process to be considered prior to the determination of key results areas and indicators of performance, which will be covered in the next chapter.

Figure 3.3. Sample Operational Analysis.

1. *Identify issues.*

Source	Operational Issues
Strategic plan	• New markets are needed in the coming year—which ones? • Additional products, tied to customers' future technological requirements, need to be developed in the coming year. • Marketing efforts need to be focused on providing technical *solutions* to customers' needs. • Long-term growth must be achieved without reducing current profitability levels. • Additional highly qualified sales and engineering personnel are needed to support future product and market requirements. • *All* parts of the organization need to have a market/customer focus.
Current operational plan	• Not enough information is available related to customers' future requirements. • R&D programs need to be focused more on [specified] technologies. • Current profitability is overly dependent on parts sales. • Facility lease comes up for renewal in the coming year. • Backlog from existing customer base is declining.
Current performance problems/opportunities	• Sales department is not receiving sufficient support from technical departments in getting bookings. • Major contract with current machining supplier is being terminated—new supplier is needed. • Materials costs are increasing with no room for short-term price increases. • Competitor X has new product that has taken part of our market share. • Competition is *not* addressing customers' *future* requirements.

Figure 3.3. Sample Operational Analysis, Cont'd.

2. *Prioritize issues.* (The following issues, with further clarification, were adopted by the executive team as having the greatest impact on the company during the coming year. Remaining issues were either delegated to specific departments for action or tabled for later review by the executive team.)
    - New markets are needed in the coming year—which ones? Potential new markets include two foreign (Europe and the Orient) and two industries (electronics and petroleum) not currently being served.
    - Additional products, tied to customers' future technological requirements, need to be developed in the coming year. A data base needs to be established to identify customer requirements.
    - R&D programs need to be focused more on [specified] technologies. These technologies are needed to replace current technology that is becoming obsolete.
    - Sales department is not receiving sufficient support from technical departments in getting bookings. Substantial sales have been lost because sales personnel were unable to respond satisfactorily to potential customers' technical concerns.
    - Current profitability is overly dependent on parts sales. The potential for continuing parts sales is diminishing and profitability needs to be made up from other products.
3. *Analyze issues.* (Following is one issue that was analyzed by members of the executive team. The other prioritized issues received similar treatment.)
    Issue:
    - New markets are needed in the coming year—which ones?
    Data/information available:
    - Demand for our products in our current markets has declined by 6 percent during the past year. Indications are that this trend will continue for the foreseeable future.
    Data/information needed:
    - Short-term foreign market potential lies in Europe and the Orient. Specific data are needed on each to determine which one to penetrate first. Data need to reflect both sales potential and possible competition.
    - Data are also needed to determine whether initial penetration will be more productive in the electronics or petroleum industry.
    Causes:
    - Current markets have matured simultaneously.
    - No provision for replacement of these markets was projected in previous plans.
    Results needed:
    - Markets selected must provide a profitable initial penetration with long-term growth potential.

Figure 3.3. Sample Operational Analysis, Cont'd.

- Markets selected must be served by existing methods of distribution.

(Analysis assignments were completed, and the following information, backed by specific data, was presented at a subsequent executive team meeting.)

- Sales potential is approximately equal (estimated $100 million annually) in Europe and the Orient. Four major competitors are firmly entrenched in Europe; only one has a significant effort in the Orient.
- Sales potential in the petroleum industry is moderate (estimated $75 million annually) but steady, with one major competitor active. In the electronics industry, sales potential is high ($150 million annually) but volatile, with six major competitors active.

4. *Summarize issues.* (Using the information provided as a result of data analysis, the executive team agreed on the following conclusions and alternative courses of action.)

Conclusion No. 1:

- Initial foreign market penetration will be in the Orient.

Alternative actions:

- Open sales office in Hong Kong, Taiwan, or Korea.
- Retain manufacturing representative firms in target countries.
- Open manufacturing operations in target countries.
- License other manufacturing outlets.

Conclusion No. 2:

- Initial new industry penetration will be in the petroleum industry with a concentration of sales efforts in Texas and Oklahoma.

Alternative actions:

- Open sales office in Texas or Oklahoma.
- Handle sales from existing sales offices.
- Retain manufacturing representative firm with petroleum industry customer base.

4

Determining Key Results Areas and Indicators of Performance

Efficiency is doing things right; effectiveness is doing right things! This statement, attributed to Peter Drucker, emphasizes the importance of selecting the *right* objectives. Operational analysis provides an excellent information base, but there are two additional elements designed to make certain that objectives are being set on the right things:

- Key results areas (KRAs) that help identify specific categories within which the most important organizational results must be achieved
- Indicators of performance that help ensure that what is being measured in the objectives represents the most important results

Figure 4.1 illustrates a commonly used approach to the setting of objectives. Following analysis, objectives are selected and then indicators are identified in order to track performance toward those objectives.

Because of the critical importance of selecting the *right* objectives, experience has demonstrated that the approach shown in Figure 4.2 is more effective. This second approach provides for a more thorough evaluation of alternatives prior to making the final decision on what objectives should be set for the coming year.

Figure 4.1. Traditional Approach to Selecting Objectives.

Figure 4.2. Recommended Approach to Selecting Objectives.

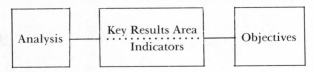

This chapter will clearly identify the purpose of key results areas and indicators of performance and show how they strengthen the selection of *right* objectives. While these are two distinctly separate elements in the operational plan, they are so closely interrelated that it is appropriate to deal with them together in one chapter. They are determined or validated at the same point in the development of the operational plan.

What Is the Purpose of Key Results Areas?

Key results areas are just that. They are areas or categories of results that are essential to effective performance in the organization. Accomplishments within these areas are necessary if the organization is to carry out its mission successfully and meet the expectations generated through the operational plan. *Key results areas do not cover everything the organization will accomplish.* They identify broad headings, usually involving cross-functional integration, under which operational objectives are developed for approval and periodic review by the board of directors and/or other higher-level body.

As preparation for selecting objectives, the determination of key results areas is a vital element that helps isolate and categorize the kinds of results needed. It reduces the likelihood of overlooking factors that, while less visible than others, may nonetheless be important to carrying out the organization's strategic plan, such as people development and organizational image. In addition, key results areas provide continuity in operational plans from one year to the next by highlighting essential performance areas, such as financial return or growth, that may not be identified as critical issues in operational analysis.

What Are Guidelines for Determining Key Results Areas?

The following basic guidelines can be used to help determine an organization's key results areas. With slight modification of the wording, these guidelines are equally applicable at the unit level. (A summary of these guidelines is shown as Figure 4.5 at the end of this chapter.)

1. *They generally will identify those four to six major areas within which the organization's performance is essential during the coming year.* Certain key results areas, such as revenue/sales and production, may be ongoing and included in every operational plan. Others, such as product line performance or capital expansion, may be included only when they are identified as critical operational issues.

2. *They will include both financial and nonfinancial areas.* While the bottom-line results are always of concern, they do not, and should not, represent the total picture of the organization's performance. Such things as product/ service quality, research and development, and people development represent an equally important part of the total picture.

3. *They will be in direct support of the organization's strategic plan.* Key results areas should be able to be linked with one or more elements of the strategic plan. They should help identify the specific results needed in the projected fiscal year to carry out the strategic plan.

4. *They will not cover the organization's entire output but will identify the critical few areas where priority efforts*

should be directed. There will be many things that will be accomplished within the organization that are essential for its ongoing performance but will not be of critical concern to the reviewing bodies. Many of these are more appropriately identified at the unit level within which the primary effort will take place. This is part of the reason for limiting the number of total organizational key results areas to from four to six. That limitation forces the planning team to determine which are the truly critical few areas where attention needs to be addressed.

5. *Most will require cross-functional effort.* At the total organization level, a key results area worthy of identification should require the active participation of two or more major functions or organizational segments. Some areas, such as product quality or organizational image, may require the active involvement of the entire organization. An exception to this guideline might be in an area of high strategic importance, such as the penetration of a major account or industry. However, even in that instance, involvement of sales, marketing, engineering, and production may be required for success.

6. *Each will be limited, generally, to two or three words and will not be measurable as stated but will contain factors that could be made measurable.* The point to keep in mind here is that these should be specific enough to identify the kinds of results needed but general enough to provide flexibility and, as appropriate, more than one specific result. Limiting key results areas to short phrases makes it easier to focus on the specific results needed.

Figure 4.3 contains several examples of key results areas that might be appropriate to many different organizations. However, this should not be seen as a prescriptive list. Some of these areas may not apply to certain organizations, and undoubtedly there are other appropriate areas that do not appear on this list. A key results area should be stated in terms that are relevant to the type of organization at hand.

Figure 4.3. Examples of Key Results Areas.

Revenue/sales
Return/profit
Growth/diversification
Market penetration
Product line performance
Productivity
New product development
People development
Organizational image
Customer relations
Quality assurance
Unit output (one or more specific areas)
Product/service design
Cost control
Cross-functional integration

What Is the Purpose of Indicators of Performance?

Indicators of performance are those measurable factors within a given key results area on which it may be worthwhile to set objectives. They generally identify *what* will be measured, not how much or by when (those come in the objectives). Their primary purpose is to identify the kind of measurable outputs desired in each of the key results areas. They provide the tangibility that is needed to lend substance to each of these areas. This is why indicators usually are identified at the same time agreement is reached on key results areas during the operational planning process. Properly selected, indicators also provide management with the most relevant information for tracking the results desired.

Indicators of performance have at least four uses in the planning process:

- Identifying a list of potential measurable factors in each key results area
- Selecting those measurable factors on which objectives should be set at this time

- Establishing specific action steps for accomplishing those objectives
- Tracking performance related to objectives and action plans

Of these, the most important purpose in operational planning is the second one, with its contribution to the selection of objectives.

A major benefit of identifying indicators of performance lies in the mind-stretching that takes place through dialogue among members of the planning team. There may be a few key results areas where the specific outcomes or objectives are so obvious that it is appropriate to move immediately into the establishment of objectives. In most areas, however, a wide variety of indicators might be used. When the planning team goes through the process of listing as many potential indicators as might be appropriate to a given key results area, the probability is substantially increased that the *right* results desired will be identified when it comes to selecting objectives. These may or may not be the ones that have been used previously or appear most obvious at the outset.

An additional value to be gained from identifying several indicators for each key results area is that those indicators can help pinpoint other factors that would be useful to track as part of the control or feedback system even if they are not included in the operational objectives. This is an important consideration in making planning a closed-loop system. Certain indicators that are not applicable to the current plan may also be useful in future planning efforts.

What Are Guidelines for Identifying Indicators of Performance?

Under normal circumstances, indicators of performance meet the following criteria: (A summary of these guidelines is shown as Figure 4.6 at the end of this chapter.)

1. *They are measurable factors, falling logically within a given key results area, on which objectives may be set.* There are many factors, such as cash flow, quality standards, and delivery schedules, that may prove very useful for tracking performance at the total organizational level but may not be especially helpful in defining objectives.

2. They may be selected from any or all of the following types:

   - *Hard numbers,* such as gross revenues, gross profit, bookings by product line, total products shipped, and number of clients served
   - *Percentages,* such as profit margins, market share, sales of new products, on-time deliveries, and new clients served
   - *Significant achievements,* such as major program completions (or milestones), certifications, industry or public recognition, and acquisitions
   - *Problems to be overcome,* such as backlog, quality deficiencies, employee skill deficiencies, and cost over-runs

3. *They identify what will be measured, not how much or in what direction.* Focusing specifically on the factor to be measured usually provides for greater objectivity in making sure the most appropriate indicator is selected. Inserting the numbers desired, before other alternatives have been considered, might lead to premature selection of the indicator (and the objective) because of its emotional appeal. For example, an indicator identified as "20 percent increase in new product sales" (which is almost an objective) might look very attractive. Selecting that as the indicator, however, might result in a failure to consider the potential deterioration of current product sales as a consequence of that amount in new products. An indicator such as "new product sales as a percentage of total product sales" might provide a more balanced perspective from which a realistic objective could be established.

4. *They represent factors that can be tracked on an ongoing basis to the extent possible.* Indicators that can only be tracked after they have been completed, such as acquisitions, are acceptable in certain areas. However, when indicators can be identified in such a way that they can be tracked as ongoing trends, such as growth in revenues or percentage of on-time deliveries, they are much more useful as a part of the total operational planning process.

Figure 4.4 contains some additional examples of indicators of performance for selected key results areas.

Figure 4.4. Examples of Indicators of Performance.

Key Results Areas	Indicators of Performance
Return/profit	Return on investment
	Percent return on sales
	Net profit before taxes (dollars)
	Percent gross margin (by product line)
Productivity	Dollars of sales per employee
	Total units produced per month (by product line)
	Percent billable time per direct employee
	Overtime as percent of payroll
People development	HRD (human resource development) investment as percent of sales
	Days of training per employee
	Percent employees using tuition reimbursement program
	Percent promotions from within
Quality assurance	Percent first-time acceptance
	Yield
	Cost of rework, scrap
	Percent error-free completions (per shift, per employee)
Cross-functional integration	Percent on-time completions
	Number of unresolved conflicts
	Average lead time on support requests
	Specific joint project agreements

In Summary

Key results areas and indicators of performance are the primary means of determining what types of operational objectives need to be set during the operational planning process. Key results areas identify those major categories within which an organization should be seeking results; indicators of performance represent those measurable factors that will identify the specific results to be achieved within each key results area. Since they are so closely related, they typically are developed at the same time. They are equally applicable at the unit level. Remember the primary purpose of identifying key results areas and indicators of performance is to enable you to establish the *right* objectives at the *right* time. This process will be addressed in the next chapter.

Figure 4.5. Guidelines for Determining Key Results Areas.

1. They generally will identify those four to six major areas within which the organization's performance is essential during the coming year.
2. They will include both financial and nonfinancial areas.
3. They will be in direct support of the organization's strategic plan.
4. They will not cover the organization's entire output but will identify the critical few areas where priority efforts should be directed.
5. Most will require cross-functional effort.
6. Each will be limited, generally, to two or three words and will not be measurable as stated but will contain factors that could be made measurable.

Figure 4.6. Guidelines for Identifying Indicators of Performance.

1. They are measurable factors, falling logically within a given key results area, on which objectives may be set.
2. They may be selected from any or all of the following types:
   - Hard numbers
   - Percentages
   - Significant achievements
   - Problems to be overcome
3. They identify what will be measured, not how much or in what direction.
4. They represent factors that can be tracked on an ongoing basis to the extent possible.

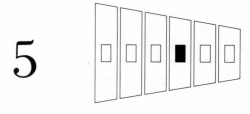

5

Selecting Operational Objectives

A frequently heard statement in the retail industry is that the three most important things to consider are location, location, and location. A board member of a client organization paraphrased that by saying that the three most important things in a profitable company are objectives, objectives, and objectives. While this is a bit of an oversimplification, there is no doubt that the selection and formulation of objectives is the focal point of any operational plan. The purpose of the first three elements of that plan—operational analysis, key results areas, and indicators of performance—is primarily to help determine what objectives should be selected. The remaining two elements—action plans and budgets—identify what needs to be done and what resources are required to ensure that objectives identified in the plan are met.

What Are Operational Objectives, and Where Do They Come From?

Operational objectives are statements of measurable results to be accomplished within the time frame of the operational plan (usually one year). At the total organizational level, this normally will be limited to the most important accomplishments projected during that period; typically, these represent effort that crosses organizational lines. They carry either specific target dates or an implied fiscal-year completion. They include, but are not limited to, projected financial results. They represent targets toward which the entire organization will be shooting as the plan progresses.

The primary sources of objectives are the conclusions reached during operational analysis and the determination of key results areas and indicators of performance. Another major source lies in the long-term objectives and integrated programs included in the strategic plan, if they have not already been reviewed during operational analysis. Since strategic plans have established the direction in which the organization should be moving over a longer period, clearly there must be some operational objectives in support of those long-term objectives and integrated programs. Another source is the personal convictions of the CEO and other key people in the organization. In addition, the board of directors, who represent the interests of the owners and are usually charged with approval or rejection of the operational plan, may provide input to the selection of objectives. For those organizations that are a part of a larger body, such as a parent company or superagency, there usually are specific requirements that need to be satisfied there as well. Managers at the unit level will be guided by objectives and action plans developed at higher levels in the organization as they prepare their unit operational plans.

How Many Objectives Should an Organization Have?

One of the purposes of establishing organizational objectives is to highlight those projected accomplishments that the CEO and the executive team should be reviewing on a regular basis. For most organizations, four to six objectives with written action plans is an appropriate number. In addition, there may be several standards of performance, related to financial and operating results, that will be tracked on a regular basis. A standard of performance represents a level of achievement to be reached and maintained on an ongoing basis that needs to be monitored but may not require

Figure 5.1. Examples of Standards of Performance.

Key Results Areas	Standards of Performance
Profit	Minimum gross margin of 35 percent
Unit output	1,000 units per shift
Product quality	Maximum three rejects per 1,000 units
Safety	Maximum one safety violation per month

a written action plan. Figure 5.1 provides some examples of standards.

It is neither desirable nor practical to write objectives on everything that should be accomplished during the period of the plan. That would simply be unmanageable. Many things are accomplished whether or not objectives are set regarding them. Written objectives should highlight those things of such critical importance that continual focus on them is required. The greater the number of objectives that are projected, the less likely it is that they will receive the amount of attention that is necessary. In addition, the paperwork generated by a large number of objectives could prove overwhelming. Objectives that are regularly reviewed at the executive level should represent those things that will have a major impact on moving the organization in the direction it must go. Furthermore, objectives at this level need to be ones that are of vital concern to all members of the executive team, not just one or two team members.

What Is the Recommended Process for Selecting Objectives?

The process for selecting objectives at the total organizational level usually takes place in a planning meeting. A coach/facilitator may guide the team through agreement on key results areas and indicators of performance that clearly need to be considered. For each key results area, one or more objectives should be identified. These may be constructed by the total planning team during the meeting itself, or individuals or subgroups within the planning team may develop proposed objectives for presentation to the entire group. In either case, objectives being considered need to be discussed at length to make certain that all pertinent factors have been considered and that the team is in agreement with what is being proposed. At this stage, it may be appropriate to identify a relatively long list of objectives as an initial effort, with the expectation that they will be reviewed a second and possibly a third time to determine which are the four to six objectives with written action plans that need to be included in the current plan. Remaining objectives on this list can be incorporated into some of the other objectives, assigned to individual members of the team for implementation at a lower level, or retained for later review and possible implementation. For example, an objective related to reducing lost-time accidents probably should be handled by the production department, with periodic reports given to the executive team if the objective is a major concern.

What Are Guidelines for Writing an Objective?

The following ground rules will aid in the formulation of objectives. Although a given objective will not necessarily conform to all these criteria, it should nonetheless be checked against each of them. Only when a conscious determination has been made that a specific guideline does not apply should it be bypassed as a factor in validating a particular objective. (A summary of these guidelines is shown as Figure 5.4 at the end of this chapter.)

1. *It starts with the word* **to** *followed by an action or accomplishment verb.* Since an objective is a statement of results, there is action involved. However, that action must clearly reflect the achievement of something, not merely the carrying out of an activity. It is important that an objective statement not reinforce activity as an end in itself. While activity may be required to accomplish the objective, that activity is more appropriately addressed in

the action plan. Thus the verb selected should focus on the result, not the activity. For example, verbs such as *complete, acquire,* or *produce* suggest accomplishment, whereas verbs such as *develop, conduct,* or *disseminate* imply activity.

2. *It specifies a single measurable result to be accomplished.* What is the one key measurement that will tell whether or not the objective has been achieved? The indicators of performance element is especially helpful in determining what that should be. Most objectives will produce a wide variety of results. It is important to select one key measurement that has an overriding indication of the desired results. For example, in evaluating market penetration, a determination needs to be made whether total dollar sales in a particular market or percent of market share is the critical indicator of performance. Either could provide the measurable result desired, but placing both into the objective could prove both cumbersome and, in some cases, incompatible (since the data base to be measured is different with each indicator). Where it may be appropriate to identify several different, but related, results, as with the above example, having more than one objective may be the solution.

3. *It specifies a target date or time span for completion.* This is an essential factor to ensure timely action. Even though many objectives have an implied plan-year completion, specific deadlines, either for the total objective or for interim steps, need to be discussed thoroughly and included in the action plan if not in the objective itself. Certain objectives (particularly those that are project-oriented), for which completion is anticipated before the end of the plan period, need to have the target date included in the objective itself. As the objective-setting process moves farther down in the organization, identifying specific target dates becomes even more important.

4. *It specifies maximum cost factors.* Before an objective is accepted, there should be a clear understanding of the resources required. These resources include time and

effort required as well as out-of-pocket costs. The value of any objective is in direct proportion to the cost of achieving it. Identifying costs associated with an objective gives an opportunity for validation through the action-planning and budgeting elements. Furthermore, it provides a more rational basis for making tradeoff decisions in determining which objectives should be pursued and which ones should be placed on hold. While it may not be feasible to identify costs on some organizational objectives, such as those in the financial area, it is important to establish some limitations on objectives related to programs, such as new products or information systems development, as guidance for implementation as well as control. Therefore, it may be considered *optional* to include the cost factor in the objective itself, particularly at the top level of the organization. The inclusion of cost limitations becomes much more practical at lower unit levels, however, where such costs are more readily identifiable. Regardless of whether or not cost is included in the objective, an examination of estimated costs is a critical consideration in determining the value of any objective.

These first four guidelines are primarily concerned with the construction of an objective statement. Our model for a well-stated objective is shown in Figure 5.2, together with three typical examples.

Figure 5.2. Model and Examples of a Well-Stated Objective.

To (action/accomplishment verb) *By* (target date/time span)
(Single measurable result)   *At* (cost in time and/or money)

- To expand agency services to include the entire county by 12/31 at a cost not to exceed $100,000
- To decrease the average cost of sales by a minimum of 5 percent effective 6/1
- To release product A to manufacturing by 9/30 at a cost not to exceed $50,000 and 5,000 engineering hours

---

The remaining four guidelines provide additional aids in the effective preparation of an organization's objectives.

5. *It is as specific and quantitative (and hence measurable and verifiable) as possible.* The objective "to increase sales to existing customers . . ." has little meaning. The objective "to increase sales to existing customers by a minimum of 10 percent . . ." provides us something specific to shoot for. Although many types of objectives lend themselves easily to quantification through the use of numbers or percentages, there are just as many that do not. This is where the indicators of performance element is especially useful. The completion of, addition of, or elimination of something is just as measurable as a set of numbers. An example would be "to complete installation of a fully automated production line by (date)." The key is in reaching agreement among the planning team on what specific measurable factors will be used.

6. *It specifies only the* **what** *and* **when;** *it avoids venturing into the* **why** *and* **how.** Once again, an objective is a statement of results to be achieved. It is not a justification for its own existence. The *why* bridge should have been crossed before the actual writing of the objective was begun. Although no one would deny that it is important that those people affected by an objective understand the reasons why it was selected, this is better handled through a verbal explanation or, if necessary, a separate statement of rationale. "To increase protective services in our service area by 10 percent . . ." identifies the result desired. "To increase protective services in our service area by 10 percent in order to accommodate the anticipated upsurge in population . . ." gets into justification, which does not belong in the actual statement of objective.

Similarly, the means of accomplishing an objective is not normally included in the objective statement. The *how* relates to the action plan (discussed in Chapter Six). The objective "to increase protective services in our

service area by 10 percent through the addition of twenty
uniformed officers . . ." suggests that there is only one
way to achieve it and thus automatically rules out other
alternatives. Most objectives may be achieved by several
acceptable approaches, the relative values of which might
vary with changing circumstances.

The important thing to bear in mind in relation to this
particular guideline is to strive toward keeping the
objective statement down to its bare essentials, which
stresses once more the simplicity aspect of preparing an
objective.

7. *It is in direct support of, or compatible with, the organization's strategic and other higher-level plans.* One of the
major reasons for an operational plan is to implement
portions of the strategic or higher-level plans that have
already been formulated. This is another check-and-
balance guideline that needs to be instituted to make
certain that the operational plan is leading the organization in a direction that is consistent with what has already
been determined. This particular guideline becomes even
more critical as organizational unit plans are developed.

8. *It is realistic and attainable but still represents a significant challenge.* This is a judgment call that the planning
team must make. Any objective set at the top level must
have a reasonably good chance of achievement with a
stretch effort. It needs to be made challenging enough so
that managers within the organization will feel good
about themselves and the organization if and when it is
achieved. At the same time, it cannot be made so difficult
that it is virtually impossible to achieve. Part of the value
in setting objectives is to provide the organization and the
managers within that organization with a sense of pride
in accomplishing something that is really worthwhile.
There is an adage that says, "Success begets success;
failure begets failure." If people within an organization
feel good about what has been accomplished, they are far
more likely to put forth additional effort to accomplish
even more. If they get the feeling that no matter how hard

they try, they can never fully succeed, their incentive for top performance quickly dissipates.

Remember, these are guidelines, not prescriptions. Guidelines need to be applied if and when they are appropriate. There may be times that some of these guidelines are not important, or they may not be applicable in a particular situation. If that decision is made with conscious awareness, it is legitimate to bypass certain guidelines. The purpose in identifying them, however, is to make certain that some of these key factors are not overlooked. Unfortunately, overlooking the obvious frequently causes problems in planning efforts. These guidelines are designed to reduce or eliminate that possibility.

Figure 5.3 (p. 60) includes several examples of improperly stated objectives that were subsequently revised. Included are some constructive comments that led to significant improvement in the original statements.

The examples in Figure 5.3 demonstrate a way in which objectives that initially are unclear or vague can be made more specific through dialogue among members of the planning team. A major responsibility of the coach/facilitator is to drive the process until the objectives stated represent clear, measurable results that reflect what the organization wishes to accomplish during that plan year. Recognize, of course, that the objectives as stated were relevant for the organizations for which they were written.

In Summary

Operational objectives represent the focal point of any operational plan. The three prior elements in the process—operational analysis, key results areas, and indicators of performance—provide the information base from which objectives are formulated. The remaining two elements—action plans and budgets—establish the means by which objectives will be met. Objectives are the principal factors by which organizational performance is measured. Therefore, it is crucial that objectives are set on the *right* things and that they are realistic and attainable.

Most well-stated objectives follow the model *to* (action/accomplishment verb), (single measurable result), *by* (target date/time span), *at* (cost). Four to six objectives with written action plans is an appropriate number at the top level of most organizations. This limitation causes top management to concentrate on the critical few accomplishments needed. Other ongoing results, such as financial, may be projected as standards of performance to be attained and maintained. At lower unit levels, a somewhat larger number of objectives and/or standards may be appropriate because of the more specific nature of the outputs required.

Once a preliminary set of operational objectives has been established, the next element to be considered is action plans, which help test and validate the objectives as well as spell out how the objectives will be accomplished. These are the subject of the next chapter.

Figure 5.3. Examples of Restated Objectives.

Original:	To increase sales from new products.
Comments:	Is your primary concern getting additional sales or getting a better balance between sales of new and existing products? Here is an opportunity to provide real guidance to your sales force on where efforts should be concentrated. In addition, is there a clear understanding of what constitutes "new products"?
Restated:	To increase the proportion of sales of new products from 10 percent to a minimum of 15 percent of total sales dollars by year's end with no increase in cost of sales.
Original:	To get a more positive image in the marketplace.
Comments:	This is a nice statement of desire, but how will you know when you get there? What has caused you to have less than the desired image? Is it a matter of product quality, deliveries, market position as compared to your competitors, image in the press, or what? If it is a combination of several factors, you may wish to commit to a specific program in which several indicators will be established and tracked through your action plan. The initiation of such a program may be a legitimate result if you have not had one before.
Restated:	To develop and implement, by March 1, an image-building program (with specified results) at a total cost, including ongoing maintenance, not to exceed $100,000.
Original:	To acquire a new company.
Comments:	Are you interested primarily in a new or expanded manufacturing capability, additional product lines, a particular service capability, access to additional markets, or a financial investment? You need to clarify the specific results you are looking for in order to develop a meaningful action plan. Is the urgency of your need such that acquisition is clearly the most appropriate course of action, rather than developing something from scratch?
Restated:	To acquire the capability of producing proven products (with minimum annual sales of $2,000,000) that support our service business by the end of the third quarter at a capital investment not to exceed $2,500,000.

Figure 5.3. Examples of Restated Objectives, Cont'd.

Original:	To make people development a priority through-out the organization.
Comments:	While this may be a noble gesture, it does not provide guidance in terms of what you really hope to accomplish through this effort. Are you specifically interested in developing new skills or capabilities or primarily in instilling a philosophy? Either approach may be appropriate, but you need to clarify the output expected.
Restated:	To have developed and implemented, in each department, a specific plan for ongoing development of people, in place by the end of the second quarter, at an annual cost not to exceed $100,000.
Original:	To develop more new products to replace those with declining sales.
Comments:	This is too vague as stated, and it gets into justification. What is the outcome you are seeking, and how will you know when you achieve it?
Restated:	To have at least three market-tested new products ready for production by the end of the second quarter at a development cost not to exceed 10,000 work hours, 2,000 hours of computer time, and $20,000 in material and equipment costs.
Original:	Study and report on alternative methods of acquiring a thirty-acre parcel adjacent to our main plant and funds required for future development purposes.
Comments:	"Study" and "report" are only activities. If the intention is to acquire the parcel, the objective should proceed with that in mind. The objective can still be modified or rejected if the initial data developed make the proposal unacceptable.
Restated:	To initiate acquisition of a thirty-acre parcel adjacent to our main plant, using the most cost-effective method available (to be determined), by November 1 at a cost of initiation not to exceed 100 work hours and $500.
Original:	Expand our technical capability by hiring new personnel and/or cross-training existing personnel.

Figure 5.3. Examples of Restated Objectives, Cont'd.

Comments:	What results are you looking for? This statement focuses more on methodology than on accomplishment. What will be an indication of successful achievement?
Restated:	To have at least three people qualified in each identified technical discipline by March 31 at a cost not to exceed two additional personnel (with related hiring costs) and 800 supervisory and training hours.
Original:	Improve clerical effectiveness.
Comments:	What is "effectiveness"? How will you know when you get there? What tells you it needs improving?
Restated:	To respond to at least 95 percent of all customer correspondence within three days, effective April 1, at no increase in clerical expense, implementation cost not to exceed 60 work hours.

Figure 5.4. Guidelines for Writing an Objective.

1. It starts with the word *to* followed by an action or accomplishment verb.
2. It specifies a single measurable result to be accomplished.
3. It specifies a target date or time span for completion.
4. It specifies maximum cost factors.
5. It is as specific and quantitative (and hence measurable and verifiable) as possible.
6. It specifies only the *what* and *when;* it avoids venturing into the *why* and *how.*
7. It is in direct support of, or compatible with, the organization's strategic and other higher-level plans.
8. It is realistic and attainable but still represents a significant challenge.

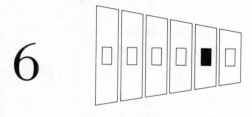

6

Preparing Action Plans

Operational objectives have been clearly established as the focal point of any operational plan. They define the results desired in specific, measurable terms. In planning a trip, the first thing to determine is the destination and the date or time of desired arrival. However, several other key decisions must be made if that trip is to be successful. These include mode of transportation, route to be followed, people to be included, accommodations to be secured, and many other considerations. While these come almost as second nature to the seasoned traveler, failure to give serious attention to even one of the key factors could result in an unsatisfactory or even disastrous trip. Drawing on this analogy, objectives are defined as the destination, while action plans describe how to get there.

What Are Action Plans?

Action plans are the specific means by which objectives are accomplished. While hundreds of books and articles have been written on the subject, each with its own terminology, action plans basically incorporate these five factors:

- The specific steps or actions required
- Who will be held accountable for seeing that each step or action is completed
- When these steps or actions are to be carried out
- What resources need to be allocated in order to carry them out

- What feedback mechanisms are needed to monitor progress within each action step

Most action plans, regardless of how simple or complex the objective is, contain between five and ten major action steps. Fewer than five indicates that insufficient consideration may have been given to the amount of effort required. More than ten suggests that more detail may have been included than is appropriate.

What Is the Purpose of an Action Plan?

The first, and most important, purpose of an action plan is to clearly *identify what has to occur* if the objective is to be accomplished. While this is obvious, the importance of this consideration becomes dramatically apparent when something is overlooked. Ironically, it is rarely the unusual occurrence that causes significant problems in the accomplishment of an objective. More frequently, such failure occurs because someone neglected to do something that is normally expected. For example, think of the number of times that an important project may have been delayed or even aborted because someone failed to make an important telephone call, a special test was overlooked, a vital piece of information or a key part failed to arrive on time, or someone who is usually reliable failed to keep a commitment. Thus an additional value of an action plan, whether at the total organizational or the unit level, is to make certain that the obvious is not overlooked.

A second purpose for an action plan is to *test and validate* the objective itself. Objectives are often established based on the results desired, with no real assurance that they are truly achievable. Once a draft objective is established, breaking it down into the smaller pieces of action that must occur if the objective is to be achieved provides an opportunity for a reality test. The action plan creates a more rational basis for determining whether:

- The objective can be reasonably accomplished within the time period projected
- The knowledge and skill necessary to carry out the plan are present in the organization
- The resources required are available or can be made available
- All necessary information is known
- There are other alternatives that need to be considered

The establishment of a detailed action plan may lead to the conclusion that the objective is unrealistic. This could result in a decision to modify the objective, modify the action plan, or postpone or even abandon the objective. The decision not to pursue an objective at this point is just as valid as a go-ahead, and it is considerably less expensive and traumatic to make such a decision before significant effort has been expended.

A third purpose for an action plan is to *serve as a communications vehicle* for others within the organization who need to contribute to, or will be affected by, what takes place. This is especially important when there are several different parts of the organization that have a distinct role to play in the achievement of the objective. Through the actual fixing of accountability on each of the action steps, there is less likelihood of delays or voids in the pursuit of the objective. Furthermore, the communication process that is involved in developing or interpreting the action plan can have a positive impact on the motivation and ownership of those who significantly influence the outcome of the objective.

What Is the Recommended Process
for Developing an Action Plan?

An action plan can be developed through one or more of the following:

Specific activities or events, not necessarily interrelated, which will lead to the accomplishment of the objective. For example, an objective related to the introduction of a new product might include separate activities related to advertising, special promotions to new customers, establishment of distribution plans, securing of appropriate financing, and any other activities that may have an impact on the effective introduction of that new product. Presumably, the successful carrying out of each of the prescribed activities, either independently or in combination with others, will lead to the successful accomplishment of the objective.

An analytical or problem-solving approach, incorporating a series of interconnected events. Through this process, the problems to be overcome or the circumstances to be changed are first clearly identified; these are then analyzed to determine appropriate courses of action, which are implemented sequentially, leading to the eventual accomplishment of the objective. For example, an objective related to increasing market share could start with an identification of principal competitors and what it is about their products and their approach that is providing them with a competitive advantage. Then specific, detailed plans can be initiated to either overcome or counterbalance these factors, leading eventually to the accomplishment of the objective.

A series of smaller or shorter-term objectives that break the objective down into smaller pieces of the larger result. A common example of this type of plan is the quarterly and monthly sales figures required to achieve an annual sales objective. These could also be broken down by region, product line, specific market, or a variety of other indicators that might be worth tracking.

Figure 6.1 shows an effective method for developing an action plan.

Figure 6.1. Action Planning Method.

---

1. Identify suggested actions in response to the following questions.
   - What activities or results are likely to contribute to the accomplishment of this objective?
   - What specific problems, obstacles, or issues need to be resolved in order to accomplish this objective?
   - What is the sequence of events required to resolve these problems?
   - What are the various ways this objective can be broken down (such as time period, department/unit, responsibility level, geographical region)?
2. Reach agreement on what combination of these actions is most appropriate for accomplishing this objective at this time.
3. Translate these actions into a series of five to ten major steps, with each step focusing on a specific result that may become an objective for an individual or unit.
4. For each action step, determine:
   - Accountability—primary and others
   - Schedule—start and completion
   - Resources—dollars and time
   - Feedback mechanisms
5. Review proposed action plans with the next lower level in the organization and others who play a key role in order to test and validate the plan, as well as to gain agreement and support.

What Is an Appropriate Action Plan Format?

We refer to this as an action plan *format*, not a *form*. A *format* is designed to identify the key factors that need to be included in the plan. It should therefore be flexible enough so that it can be modified to meet the information needs of the managers using it. A *form*, in contrast, is usually designed to respond to a prescribed reporting system and consequently tends to be more rigid. Figure 6.2 shows a very simple format that can be used in laying out a meaningful action plan. The purpose of preparing an action plan using this type of format is to provide the *visibility* needed to get the job done in the most effective and efficient manner. Therefore, don't create a piece of paper that inhibits this process.

Figure 6.2. Action Plan Format.

Action Plan

Objective:

Action Steps	Accountability		Schedule		Resources		Feedback Mechanisms
	Primary	Others	Start	Complete	Dollars	Time	

Source: The Executive Guide to Operational Planning by George L. Morrisey, Patrick J. Below, and Betty L. Acomb. San Francisco: Jossey-Bass. Copyright © 1988. Permission to reproduce hereby granted.

Here is a brief description of what is included under each of the headings shown in Figure 6.2:

- *Objective.* The specific operational objective for which the action is being prepared.
- *Action steps.* The five to ten major actions or events required to achieve the objective.
- *Accountability.* The specific individuals (or units) who will be held accountable for seeing that the action step is carried out. *Primary* represents the one who has ultimate accountability for completion of the step; *others* represents anyone else with a key role to play in that particular step.
- *Schedule.* This shows the total time frame within which the action step is to be carried out. *Start* identifies when the action must begin; *complete* identifies when that action or event must be completed.
- *Resources.* The total estimated costs for completing each of the action steps. *Dollars* includes all costs other than employee time, such as equipment, materials, systems, and supplies: *time* covers the amount of employee time (usually in hours or days) required to complete each action step. Time is separated from dollars in order to provide data for scheduling and for determining staffing needs.
- *Feedback mechanisms.* This refers to the specific methods that are available (or need to be developed) for providing the information required to track progress within each step. Feedback mechanisms can be as simple as an informational meeting or memo or as involved as the development of an information system to provide a report.

While the data included on this worksheet may be condensed when the final operational plan is prepared, completion of such a worksheet will help ensure that key factors in the plan have not been overlooked. Figures 6.3 and 6.4 show possible action plans for top-level objectives. These plans are for illustrative purposes only and will not necessarily be appropriate for other, similar objectives.

Figure 6.3. Sample Action Plan for a Medium-Sized Manufacturing Company.

Action Plan

Objective: To increase productivity from 120 to 130 units per hour by December 31 at an implementation cost not to exceed $35,000. (This presumes no increase in ongoing production cost.)

Action Steps	Accountability		Schedule		Resources		Feedback Mechanisms
	Primary	Others	Start	Complete	Dollars	Time	
1. Complete detailed study of manufacturing operations, identifying specific areas of potential productivity improvement	Industrial Engr.	Unit Suprvs.	1/15	1/31	$2,000	80 hrs	Completed report with recommendations
2. Establish and monitor quarterly targets for productivity improvement: • First quarter: 122 • Second quarter: 124 • Third quarter: 127 • Fourth quarter: 130	V.P. of Mfg.		1/1 4/1 7/1 10/1	3/31 6/30 9/30 12/31			Quarterly results report and review meetings
3. Increase production volume: • Punch press: 10% • Assembly: 8% • Final inspection: 8%	Production Supt.	Unit Suprvs.	2/15	3/31	3,000	100 hrs	Weekly and monthly production reports
4. Reduce out-of-stock levels of critical materials from 10% to max. 5%	Purch. Mgr.		3/1	6/30	2,000	80 hrs	Summary of inventory management report
5. Reduce equipment maintenance downtime from 15% to max. 7%	Maint. Suprv.	Unit Suprvs.	3/1	9/15	4,000	120 hrs	Equipment performance report
6. Increase long production runs from 40% to 60% of scheduled runs	Sched. Suprv.	Unit Suprvs.	3/1	9/30	1,000	120 hrs	Monthly production meeting—analysis of production schedule mix
7. Complete supervisory training for ten manufacturing unit supervisors in areas of performance measurement and employee motivation	Production Supt.	Training Coord.	6/1	12/15	5,000	200 hrs	Memo from training director
8. Reduce total scrap levels from 4% to max. 2%	Quality Assur. Mgr.	Unit Suprvs.	9/1	11/15	5,000	80 hrs	Monthly quality scrap and rework summary

Figure 6.4. Sample Action Plan for a Medium-Sized City.

Action Plan

Objective: To reduce the number of vehicular accidents on city streets by a minimum of 5% over prior year's level at an implementation cost not to exceed $15,000.

Action Steps	Accountability Primary	Others	Schedule Start	Complete	Resources Dollars	Time	Feedback Mechanisms
1. Determine locations of highest incidence and select those with highest potential for improvement	Traffic Engr.	Police	9/1	9/15		40 hrs	Special report summarizing high-incidence areas
2. Set up ad hoc committee to analyze and recommend corrective actions, including but not limited to: • Education • Increased surveillance • Traffic control equipment • Possible rerouting	Asst. City Mgr.	Traffic Engr. Police City Plng. Citizens	9/15	10/15	$ 500	60 hrs	Names of committee members; first meeting minutes
3. Establish information/motivation plan for police officers	Police		10/15	11/15	250	20 hrs	Copy of plan
4. Inform City Council, City Mgr., other related departments, and the media about plans and progress	Asst. City Mgr.		10/15	12/15	250	20 hrs	Memo outlining plans and progress
5. Test proposed plans in selected locations	Traffic Engr.	Police	11/15	12/15	500	100 hrs	Monthly accident report
6. Establish monitoring system	Asst. City Mgr.	Data Proc. Traffic Engr. Police	11/15	Ongoing	1,000	100 hrs	Copy of special detailed accident report for selected areas
7. Implement plans	Traffic Engr.	Police Pub. Rel.	1/1	Ongoing	1,000	40 hrs per mo	Memo to announce kickoff date for new system
8. Evaluate and modify implementation plans	Asst. City Mgr.	Ad hoc comm.	4/1	5/1	500	60 hrs	Quarterly management meeting to evaluate results

What Factors Need to Be Reviewed
in the Formulation of an Action Plan?

There are an almost infinite number of factors that can impact the way an action plan is developed. Many of these will have been addressed during operational analysis. However, reviewing them at this stage provides another opportunity to make certain critical considerations are not being overlooked. Here are a few of the more frequently identified factors for review. The most useful list, however, is the one that is uniquely relevant to each organization.

- *Strategic and/or operational plan impact.* In addition to its contribution to the accomplishment of the specific related objective, an action plan frequently will have significant impact, positive or negative, on other portions of the strategic or operational plans. Whether multiple benefit can be derived from a specific action step should be a consideration in the selection of that step. For example, doing a market/competitor analysis in support of an objective to increase market share may also provide significant data that would help in new product development. Conversely, an advertising campaign supporting a new product needs to be evaluated to make certain that it does not significantly depress sales of existing products, resulting in an overall loss of market share.
- *Financial impact.* The impact on the bottom line is a major consideration as action plans are developed. This can relate to both long-term and short-term revenue, as well as to both capital and operating expense. For example, a new product line that requires a substantial tooling investment might have a significantly different priority when interest rates are high than when they are low. Short-term cash flow implications also may help determine when portions of a particular plan should be implemented.
- *Resource availability.* While related to financial impact, this is nonetheless a distinctly different type of consideration. Resources could include such things as skilled

personnel, raw materials, information flow, distribution channels, and other resources that may be in short or plentiful supply whether or not the financial wherewithal is available. For example, relocating a portion of a company's operations from an area that has a shortage of skilled labor to an area where such labor is in greater supply may make eminently good sense even if the initial financial investment is considerably more.

- *State of the art.* When action plans involve a technology that is rapidly changing, either creating or staying abreast of the current state of the art in that technology becomes a critical consideration. This may require attention in the plan to such things as research and development, information systems, market and industry research, and other factors that will reduce the likelihood that portions of the plan will become obsolete. An organization need not be on the leading edge of technology to use this factor to advantage. For example, IBM is rarely, if ever, in the forefront of technological breakthroughs in its industry. However, its ability to stay on top of technology, moving into key products once the technology has been proven, is legendary in the industry.

- *Environmental conditions.* Factors such as climate, weather, natural resources, and peculiar geographical circumstances are examples of environmental conditions over which an organization has little or no control but which may substantially impact certain action plans. An organization located in a river valley in the northern part of the country that does not consider the potential impact of a heavy winter snowfall in nearby mountains may find itself getting wetter than it would like during the spring thaw.

- *Political sensitivities.*Certainly those organizations that are in the public sector, that do business with organizations in the public sector, or that have significant investments in other countries had better remain alert to the political trends affecting their operations. In politics, nothing is forever. Those organizations that are prepared to respond quickly to major political shifts are much more likely to be successful in this arena. However, there are other political considerations, perhaps a bit more subtle, that impact *every* organization, regardless of where it does business. These include the influence of key customers, board members, parent organization, key executives, regulatory agencies, the media, and public opinion in general. For example, organizations that are involved in nuclear or weapons research, toxic waste, or care for the elderly or are doing business in politically sensitive parts of the world (such as South Africa during the mid 1980s) recognize the need to adjust plans accordingly if they are to survive. The decision to proceed with a plan of action that contains steps that are either highly pleasing or displeasing to some of these groups deserves careful consideration.

- *Contractual requirements.* Customer or labor contracts, as well as other legal commitments, may require a different course of action than would be appropriate if such contracts did not exist. For example, a labor contract may contain a clause requiring advance notice of a facility relocation.

- *Calendar- or fiscal-year events.* Such events as stockholder meetings, industry-wide new-model introduction (auto-mobiles or fashions, for example), major holidays, and strategic and operational plan submission deadlines may play a significant role in the way a particular action plan is developed.

- *Contingency plans.* Finally, no planning process is complete without a provision for contingency or backup plans in case the unexpected happens. For plans with high impact, a part of plan preparation needs to be devoted to "what if" analysis. This should result in identification of alternatives to be considered in the event the primary plan goes awry. The review process in results management provides for plan modification when that becomes necessary.

The purpose in describing these various factors is to draw attention to the need for identifying special considerations when developing action plans. As indicated above, there are many other factors that may be appropriate to a particular type of organization. Creating a list of these factors should not deter managers from proceeding with their plans, but it should reduce the likelihood of their being surprised as plans evolve.

In Summary

Action plans describe the means by which objectives are accomplished. They include the specific steps or actions required, who is accountable, when the steps will be carried out, and what resources are needed. They are developed using one or a combination of specific activities or events, an analytical or problem-solving approach, or a series of smaller or shorter-term objectives. In addition to determining how objectives are accomplished, action plans help test and validate the objectives and serve as a communications vehicle for others in the organization. This is also an appropriate place, because of the level of detail required, to review several special considerations, such as financial impact, state of the art, and political sensitivities. Finally, action plans provide important information for preparing and integrating budgets, which are covered in the next chapter.

7

Integrating Budgets
with the Operational Plan

"Budgets are budgets and plans are plans and never the twain shall meet" should never be a clarion cry in any organization. Where both exist, the plan and the budget need to be closely intertwined or budgeting will quickly turn into a numbers game and planning will be seen as an academic exercise. A basic premise in this book is that budgets must be integrated with operational plans and vice versa. The budget decision-making and reconciliation process must be closely linked to the previous five elements in the operational plan. In fact, the data that are generated through the first five elements provide an excellent information base for the preparation and management of realistic budgets.

First of all, there is a distinction between budgets and budgeting. A *budget* is a document that expresses the operational plan in detailed financial terms. Its purpose is to provide a pre-established financial framework within which the organization can achieve its objectives. *Budgeting* is the ongoing process of determining, allocating, and controlling financial resources required to attain the organization's objectives. This chapter will focus primarily on *budgeting* as a management tool in developing and carrying out the organization's operational plan. Although budgets are a natural outcome of this process, this chapter will not address the preparation or administration of budgets (see the Annotated Bibliography for specific references in this area). This chapter establishes the importance of linkage between plans and budgets and shows how this linkage will strengthen *both* the plan and the budget.

What Is the Purpose of Budgeting?

The primary purposes of budgeting as a management tool, the final element in the operational planning process, are:

- To optimize the use of limited financial resources to achieve desired results
- To provide ongoing visibility of financial performance to plan
- To focus on the priority areas that have greatest financial significance to the organization
- To provide an additional forum for communication, participation, and involvement in the planning and budgeting process

As such, budgeting becomes a vital link in the total operational planning process. It ensures the integration of the budget with the other elements of the operational plan.

What Is the Role of Budgeting in Operational Planning?

As pointed out earlier, the process of budgeting (resulting in the development of a total budget with supporting detailed budgets) is the final element in the operational planning process. It completes the cycle by ensuring that objectives and action plans can be accomplished with available financial resources. Without careful attention to integrating budgeting as a key part of the planning process, organizations run a strong risk of either overcommitting or undercommitting on what can reasonably be accomplished during the plan year.

There are three primary budgeting roles in the operational planning process:

1. To *determine* the level of financial resources required to achieve plan objectives
2. To *allocate* available financial resources to ensure their optimum use in achieving plan objectives
3. To *control* the use of available resources to ensure the achievement of plan objectives

Thus, the budgeting process provides an ongoing series of checks and balances between the achievement of objectives and the availability and use of resources. Management's responsibilities in carrying out these three roles represent the focus in the remainder of this chapter. However, there are some concerns that need to be addressed to ensure an effective budgeting process.

What Keeps the Budgeting Process from Being More Effective?

Logic clearly suggests that the integration of the budgeting process with the operational plan is both obvious and desirable. Why does there appear to be difficulty in following this logical progression, and how can the process proposed here effectively overcome this difficulty? Below are some typical reactions that reflect some of these difficulties, together with a rationale for addressing them.

"Why can't our managers submit realistic budgets based on what they truly expect to accomplish, rather than wish lists?" This typical quote from a CEO or financial executive reflects a legitimate concern about the way many budget submissions are prepared. Some managers either don't have an adequate data base for preparation of their budgets or prepare them without enough careful thought. This frequently leads to unrealistic budgets, with the inevitable result that the final approved budget bears little resemblance to what was initially submitted.

There is a high probability that more realistic budgets will be developed when specific objectives and action plans are identified *before* preparing budgets—that is, when the

- Selected budget adjustments are based on data derived by managers from tracking indicators of performance.
- Budget adjustments from above are made selectively rather than across the board.
- When budgets are adjusted (either at the beginning or during the course of the plan year), objectives and/or action plans are modified accordingly, and vice versa.

How Is the Total Organization's Budget Determined?

Primary sources of information needed in the determination of the budget include:

- Estimates of resources required to achieve the organization's objectives and carry out the related action plans
- The application of historically reliable standards and ratios as they apply to budget estimates
- Reference to previous budget estimates and performance to those estimates

The importance of estimating the cost of achieving objectives and, in particular, of carrying out action plans has been stressed in Chapters Five and Six. The amount of time and effort required helps determine the number and types of personnel needed. Out-of-pocket cost estimates help establish other resource requirements. The more accurate these estimates are, the more realistic will be the projected budget. Therefore, it becomes increasingly important to ensure a clear understanding at all levels of what resources are required to achieve desired results. Furthermore, when succeeding levels of management estimate the resources required to carry out their portions of the plan, there is a built-in set of checks and balances to test budgetary validity. For example, in support of an organizational objective to introduce a new product line, a production superintendent may estimate 1,000 hours and $5,000 to produce a working prototype. However, inputs from design engineering, manufacturing engineering, and the test laboratory may suggest costs that are several times that amount. Examination of each portion of the plan by the related managers provides a basis for increasing the accuracy of these estimates as well as eliminating, modifying, or adding specific action steps together with their related costs. A revised estimate of 1,800 hours and $7,500 may turn out to be a more realistic budget projection. The projections from this production superintendent are then combined with estimates from other contributing units, such as marketing, sales, purchasing, and tooling, to determine what the total budget should be to support that specific objective.

In addition to the cost estimates generated as a result of analyzing objectives and action plans, there are certain historically reliable standards and ratios that have been established within the organization or the industry that can help determine resources required. Examples of these are shown in Figure 7.1. This aspect of budgeting is an excellent illustration of integration within the operational plan, since these standards or ratios can also be used as indicators of performance to further test and refine their accuracy. For example, since sales volume per salesperson typically is an important ratio, a specific indicator of performance can be set up, followed by an objective and action plan to both meet the target and track the validity of this standard. Then, in the following year's budget, there would be a far better understanding of this standard as an indicator for establishing sales targets.

A major responsibility of the CEO and the executive team is to review the budget estimates in light of total results expected and resource availability. When these are compatible, the budgeting process is relatively easy. However, this rarely is the case the first time around. When, as is usually the situation, there are significant differences between the budget and rest of the operational plan, managerial judgment must be applied to one or a combination of the following courses of action:

- Selecting alternative action plans that can achieve the same results at lower cost

Figure 7.1. Examples of Standards and Ratios.

Sales and Marketing	Manufacturing
Minimum sales volume per salesperson Sales expense as percent of total sales Unit sales by product line and sales territory	Ratio of direct to indirect personnel Materials cost as percent of total cost Total units per work hour

Sales and Marketing

Minimum sales volume per
 salesperson
Sales expense as percent of total
 sales
Unit sales by product line and
 sales territory

Financial

Percent return on sales
Debt to equity
Accounts receivable aged

Human Resources

Dollars of sales per employee
Total training dollars as percent
 of sales
Total percent increase in employee compensation
Employee benefits as percent of
 total compensation

Manufacturing

Ratio of direct to indirect
 personnel
Materials cost as percent of total
 cost
Total units per work hour

Distribution

Percent gross margin
Inventory turnover
Percent mark up by product line

Services

Percent billable time per direct
 employee
Percent client retention
Number of new clients per
 month

Retail

Dollar profit per square foot of
 floor space
Advertising as percent of sales

- Modifying budget estimates, based on the points of view of other experienced managers
- Securing/providing additional resources to those originally projected
- Modifying, postponing, or eliminating certain objectives and/or action steps

While this list may appear simplistic, the process of arriving at the final decisions may be painful, arduous, and time-consuming. Managerial decision making usually involves making important tradeoffs. Even with completely accurate and reliable information, budgetary decisions represent a managerial gamble. The planning process leading up to these decisions must be designed to make the odds as favorable as possible.

How Are Resources Allocated
Through the Budgeting Process?

While the same process will apply if budget estimates are lower than the amount of resources available, the allocation process is more likely to be applied when budget estimates are considerably higher. The assumption being made here is that submitted budget estimates are as accurate as possible. The information developed by going through the planning process should improve the accuracy and reliability of budget projections. If the philosophy and process described thus far in this book have been followed, the need for simply crunching numbers in the budgeting process should be minimized.

There are three major considerations that should be kept in mind as the allocation process evolves:

- That sufficient resources are allocated to bring about the achievement of priority objectives.
- That there is a balance between operational and long-term objectives.
- That there is adequate funding for critical support operations such as accounting, maintenance, safety, and training. These operations may have only an indirect impact on the first two considerations.

Some of the more difficult decisions that may have to be made during budget review time come in relation to balancing operational and long-term objectives. Unfortunately, there is often a tendency to make planning decisions with a philosophy that suggests: this year we are concerned about this year; next year we will be concerned about next year; the year after doesn't exist. Furthermore, many reward systems, particularly incentive or bonus plans, tend to reinforce that philosophy. When faced with a choice between investing in new product development (which may not produce revenue until two or three years in the future) and making the same investment in current sales and production, the urgency of the bottom line favors the latter action. At this point, the CEO's leadership is especially critical to make certain that urgency does not take precedence over importance. This may mean that certain long-term objectives, in such areas as facility expansion or technology advancement, will have to be declared untouchable, even at the expense of desired short-term gains.

Finally, when the budget crunch is on, there is a tendency to look first at making cuts in those support areas that do not make a direct bottom-line contribution. This is legitimate to a certain extent. Drastically reducing a revenue-producing capability while maintaining a large overhead operation could be a fast ticket to organizational oblivion. However, the reverse of that could be equally disastrous. One company we know reduced the size of its accounting staff, including major cuts in the credit and accounts receivable operations, in order to increase its sales force. The result was a substantial increase in sales but a much greater increase in uncollectible accounts and aged receivables. Once again, balanced decision making is the key to success in the budget allocation and reconciliation process.

There is no easy formula for making budget adjustments. An across-the-board cut may be the simplest approach administratively, but it does not take advantage of the information generated through an effective planning process. Furthermore, it encourages "creative" budgeting among managers whose survival instincts prevail over consideration of what is best for the total organization. Selective adjustments among many worthwhile budget alternatives are some of the most difficult decisions executives must make. Maybe that's one of the reasons they get, and deserve, those fabulous salaries.

How Does Control Fit into the Budgeting Process?

Once a budget has been determined and allocation and reconciliation decisions have been made, the important managerial role of budgetary monitoring and control comes into play. The key concern is whether objectives are being achieved within the allocated resources. If they are, there is no problem. However, when results are less than anticipated, there may be a number of reasons for this and management has to exercise the appropriate action. Figure 7.2 illustrates the important relationship between operational planning and results management, with particular emphasis on the role of budgets. Variances between actual performance and planned performance are identified from the management reports. These variances can be addressed by adjusting one or a combination of objectives, action plans, or budgets, or by taking corrective action related to people or performance problems. Regardless of which options are selected, the budgeting process is an integral part of both the operational plan and the results management components of the Integrated Planning Process.

As Figure 7.2 depicts, adjustments may come from one or a combination of four courses of action:

- Adjust the budget estimated (this can be either up or down depending on the results being achieved).
- Adjust the action plans.
- Adjust the objectives (again, either up or down).
- Address a particular performance/people problem that may exist in the organization.

In Summary

Budgets are an integral part of the operational plan. An effective budgeting process is needed to ensure that budgets and plans are integrated throughout the operational planning process. Our emphasis has been on the budgeting *process,* not the preparation of budgets (see the Annotated Bibliography for references in this area). Budgeting is defined as the ongoing process of determining, allocating (including reconciling with the operational plan), and controlling financial resources in order to attain the organization's objectives.

Figure 7.2. Budget Control Process.

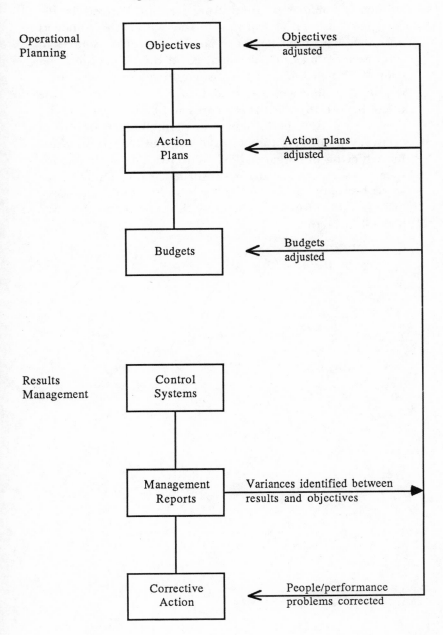

Effective application of the budgeting process is dependent on managers submitting realistic budgets in the first place, as well as learning to stay within these budgets once they have been set. There are three primary sources of information that can aid managers in the preparation and control of their budgets: a realistic estimate of the resources required to achieve objectives and carry out action plans, the use of historically reliable standards and budget ratios, and a review of budget performance to plan. Budget allocation decisions are made on the basis of meeting the requirements for achieving the organization's objectives, balancing short-term and long-term needs, and ensuring adequate funding for critical support areas. A final role in the budget process, managerial control of resources, will be covered in the third book of this series.

8

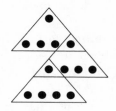

Operational Planning
at the Unit Level

The success of any operational planning effort is in direct proportion to the degree that such plans are developed and implemented at the middle and first line management levels. The emphasis in this book thus far has been on clarification of the six operational plan elements, with primary application of the process at the senior executive level. This is appropriate, since the senior executive team must set the stage for determining what the total organization should accomplish during the next plan year. However, those plans have little value unless they are translated into specific unit plans and the key people within those units accept the responsibility for carrying them out. A symphony conductor will get beautiful music only when the strings, brass, woodwinds, and percussion play the right notes at the right time. This is equally true in any other organization. This chapter focuses on making the operational planning process come alive at the unit level, with the expectation that these plans will be translated into meaningful action that will lead to the desired results. The term *unit*, as used here, refers to any discrete portion of a larger organization, including, but not limited to, a division, department, section, district, office, or, in some instances, one-person operation.

What Are the Benefits of Unit Operational Planning
to Middle and First Line Managers?

For middle and first line managers to accept the responsibility for doing an effective job of unit planning, they must perceive that the effort required will result in a benefit for them individually and for their units, as well as for the total organization. If their perception is that planning is just more work with no direct payoff for them, the results of such planning are likely to fall far short of what senior management wants or expects. Some individual and group benefits of unit and operational planning are:

- *A feeling of being in control.* Unit operational planning provides a vehicle for both understanding and influencing the total organization's plan and those portions of that plan for which these managers will be held accountable. The assumption here is that those who are on the firing line are more likely to know what is required to achieve desired organizational results than those who may be several levels removed from the action. Furthermore, they are far more likely to be committed to carrying out organizational plans if they have had something to say about their creation. In addition, unit managers stand a much better chance of getting approval for the resources they need if they have a clear set of objectives and action plans that support those resource requirements.

- *More productive use of personal and unit time.* Many middle and first line managers become extremely frustrated over the amount of time spent by them personally and by people within their units in firefighting, rework, and responding to unexpected changes rather than in ongoing productive effort. While a certain amount of such activity is inevitable, the development of meaningful unit plans provides greater opportunity for anticipating problems and changes as well as for making tradeoff decisions when it comes to the priority use of managerial and employee time. Agreement on the results that need to be achieved by all people affecting that unit's work increases the probability that individual and group efforts will have a greater payoff for them, their units, and the total organization.

- *Improved communication and coordination with others.*
  Each middle and first line manager has several "others"
  with whom planned and coordinated effort is a necessity.
  These include employees, people in other parts of the
  organization, higher-level management, suppliers, and
  customers. The establishment of clear unit operational
  plans, with particular emphasis on objectives and action
  plans, identifies what roles these "others" need to be
  playing in order for the planned results to be achieved.
  Employees reporting to that manager, in particular, will
  be able to use the same process in planning their own
  work. This reduces the potential for confusion and
  miscommunication when it comes to coordinating these
  efforts. Furthermore, it provides a sound basis for getting
  the active involvement and commitment of these employees as well as for establishing clear accountability for
  results. In addition, unit action plans provide a means for
  clearly identifying others with whom early coordination
  and mutual support are essential for plan implementation.

In short, unit operational plans allow middle and front
line managers to concentrate more on their management
responsibilities while providing them with a clear sense of
worthwhile accomplishment.

When and How Are Unit Operational Plans Developed?

Although the natural sequence in planning suggests
that the operational plan for the total organization precedes
that of the individual unit, portions of the unit planning
process can and should be initiated before the total plan is
finalized. This is especially important since information
generated at the unit level is likely to influence the content of
the total organization's plan. Therefore, unit planning that is
done in concert with that of the total organization will provide
for greater consistency, more realistic cross-functional
integration, and a greater sense of ownership on the part of

people within the various units. This leads to a much more cohesive plan for the total organization.

The various elements of the operational plan described earlier in this book have equal applicability at the unit level. Unit plans, of course, will be somewhat narrower in scope and will cover more detail than is appropriate at the senior level. Following are some specific considerations that may be useful in developing unit plans:

- *Unit roles and missions* provide a strong foundation for the development of unit operational plans. Since mission is primarily a strategic planning element, it is not being addressed specifically in the main body of this book. A special supplement is included at the end of this chapter as a guide for those units that may not have such a statement in place already. Those units with such a document may find it useful to check theirs against the guidelines provided to make certain nothing has been overlooked.

- *Information from the executive level* that is disseminated before plans are completed provides insight into where priority efforts should be directed. Early dissemination of this information also provides opportunity for constructive feedback and content input from the unit level to the executive level. Responsibility for this dissemination usually belongs to executive team members for units under their jurisdiction.

- *Unit issues and expectations* may be identified from the issues, conclusions, and recommendations that are spelled out during the senior team's operational analysis. Figure 8.1 shows several examples of organizational issues identified earlier, with potential related issues that need to be addressed at the unit level.

    In addition to issues that may come as a result of executive-level operational analysis, each unit may wish to go through its own operational analysis in order to identify, prioritize, analyze, and summarize issues, conclu-

Figure 8.1. Unit Issue Identification.

Total Organizational Issue	Potential Unit Issues
Need for new product focus	Sales—new product sales incentives Marketing—greater predictability of market trends R&D—targeted new product development Manufacturing—retooling requirements
Declining margins	Sales—excessive sales expense Marketing—improper pricing Purchasing—excessive raw material costs Manufacturing—excessive production costs
Decrease in client population	Program Management—additional client services Human Resources—retraining of selected personnel Field Services—closing/consolidating selected offices
Poor delivery performance	Sales—unrealistic delivery commitments Distribution—excessive turnaround time Manufacturing—delays in production flow

sions, and alternative courses of action that need to be addressed in the unit plan.

• *A hierarchy of objectives and action plans* may identify specific issues, key results areas, indicators of performance, objectives, and action plans that need to be addressed at the unit level. *Hierarchy,* in this case, refers to the interlocking of higher-level with unit objectives. Frequently, what may be identified as one step in the action plan supporting a higher-level objective will, in turn, become a key results area or an objective at a lower level in the organization. Figure 8.2 shows two examples of a descending hierarchy of objectives that are appropriate at different unit levels.

Figure 8.2. Examples of Hierarchy of Objectives.

Private Sector

Corporate: To develop one new product line for marketing in the next fiscal year.

    Marketing: To establish and implement a marketing plan for the new product line by (date) at (cost).

        Market Analysis: To complete an analysis of the new line's market potential by (date) at (cost).

    Manufacturing: To initiate full production of the new product line by (date) at (cost).

        Tooling: To complete tooling required for new product line by (date) at (cost).

Public Sector

Agency: To develop and implement a decentralized public information service in the next fiscal year.

    Field Services Division: To establish and implement a development plan for the new service by (date) at (cost).

        Field Analysis: To complete an analysis of public demand for the new service by (date) at (cost).

    Program Management: To provide real-time access to field units on current program status effective (date) at (cost).

        Information Systems: To develop and install a computer program providing real-time access on current program status by (date) at (cost).

    Examining the hierarchy of objectives will also clearly identify where cross-functional planning and coordination may be required. This increases the probability of organizational integration of the operational planning process. It encourages the establishment of win-win relationships among various organizational units.

- *Classification of objectives* into regular/routine, problem-solving, and innovative is another method for identifying unit outputs. George Odiorne (see the Annotated Bibliography) developed a concept of these three levels of objectives as shown in Figure 8.3. At the base of the pyramid are the regular, or routine, objectives, which describe primarily the normal, ongoing outputs of the particular unit. These may also be stated as standards of performance, as described in Chapter Five. The next

Figure 8.3. Three Classes of Objectives.

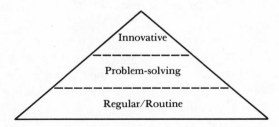

higher level, problem-solving objectives, represents those outputs designed to fix any of the regular objectives that may not be satisfactorily accomplished, as well as chronic problems that may exist. The highest level, innovative objectives, represents outputs that are above and beyond normal expectations of the unit. These might include such things as developing a new service or product, significantly improving quality, or introducing new and more effective or efficient methods. These objectives would, of course, still be in response to data generated in earlier parts of the operational planning process. The reason these objectives are shown in a pyramid is to portray graphically that the higher-level objectives generally represent a higher level of both payoff and risk. In addition, while acknowledging the potentially greater importance of the higher-level objectives, the pyramid establishes a position that these may not be done at the expense of the normal unit expectations that provide the foundation for unit output.

How Does Top Management Know When There Is an Effective Unit Operational Planning Process in Place?

The obvious answer to this question, of course, is when the results projected in response to the total organization's operational plan are properly achieved and there is evidence of strong support throughout the organization. However, more specifically, there are some clear indications that the process is working properly. These include such things as:

- Each member of the senior executive team has a clear plan for making the process work within his or her jurisdiction.
- There is evidence that all six elements within the operational planning process are being addressed at each unit level. Some elements, such as operational analysis and key results areas, may not require significant effort at lower levels, since much of that data may have been predetermined at higher levels.
- There is evidence that planning decisions involve team members at the unit level, not just the unit leader.
- Action plans at the unit level include provision for cross-functional coordination as needed. Furthermore, there is evidence that coordination is, in fact, taking place.
- Random inquiries by members of top management, of employees at all levels, reveal an understanding by those employees of total organizational objectives as well as those of their own units.

In Summary

Operational planning, to be truly successful, is dependent on the active support of units within an organization. For this support to happen consistently, middle and first line managers must perceive such benefits as:

- A feeling of being in control
- More productive use of personal and unit time
- Improved communication and coordination with others

The process for developing unit operational plans is similar to that for the total organization, although unit plans will be narrower in scope and will cover more detail. Unit plan development can be facilitated through:

- Development of unit roles and missions (see supplement to this chapter)
- Dissemination of information from the executive level
- Identification of unit issues and expectations in support of those at the top
- Review of the objectives and action plans hierarchy
- Classification of objectives into routine/regular, problem-solving, and innovative

Finally, members of top management need to reinforce the importance of involvement and commitment by middle and first line managers in the operational planning process. Without their active support, operational planning is unlikely to produce the desired organizational results.

SUPPLEMENT TO CHAPTER EIGHT

Developing Unit Roles and Missions

As indicated in the main portion of this chapter, a statement of roles and missions for each discrete work unit is an important foundation document in the development of a unit operational plan. Naturally, this must be in support of the total organization's mission. However, there are some distinct differences that apply to the statement of a specific unit. One requirement is that each unit be clearly separate from each other. There should be no two units within a total organization with identical roles and missions. Otherwise, there is an open invitation for duplication of services or, what may be worse, effort gap.

Why Should There Be a Statement of Roles and Missions for Each Separate Unit?

There are several reasons that each unit should have its own statement of roles and missions. Some of the more critical factors are:

- To ensure that all critical work required is accomplished and accountability is established for it, thus avoiding the problems that occur when everyone assumes that somebody else is doing it
- To reduce, if not eliminate, the likelihood of duplication of effort
- To ensure that individual employees within the organization clearly see the relationship between what they are doing and the apparent reasons for the existence of the total organization
- To ensure that organizational effort is being expended on work that clearly contributes to, and does not detract from, the economic welfare of the total organization
- To reduce the likelihood of jurisdictional disputes among related organizational units

- To serve as a forum for resolution of misunderstandings or disputes within each unit as well as among related units

While a clear statement of roles and missions will not guarantee appropriate addressing of these various factors, the absence of such a statement will inevitably lead to some of the negative consequences implied. In addition, of course, a valid statement of roles and missions is the baseline from which all unit objectives should be drawn. In other words, any objective accepted by a manager should be in direct support of the unit's statement of roles and missions; otherwise, serious questions should be raised as to whether any significant effort should be devoted to that objective.

Where Does That Statement Come From?

Ideally, a clear, concise, and comprehensive statement of mission for the total organization provides the basis for roles and missions statements of smaller units within it. In fact, if no organization-wide statement exists, each manager must create one, at least conceptually, before the unit's roles and missions can be defined.

A good starting place is at the department level—or whatever the level is called at which functional separation begins (with such groupings as production, marketing, engineering, finance, administration). For organizations that are structured in some other way, such as by program or geographical area, the starting place should be at whatever is the equivalent of a department. Each department head should prepare such a statement with the help of other key managers in that department. These then need to be shared with peer-level managers in an open forum. Working together, these managers can help one another refine the statements for their departments while reducing the likelihood of significant overlap, significant gap, or jurisdictional disputes. As appropriate, this same process can be carried on down through each organizational unit. The degree to which other managers outside a unit need to be involved will vary,

Figure 8.4. Clarifying Organizational Unit Roles and Missions.

---

1. What business is the total organization in? Why does it exist?
2. What business is our organizational unit in?
3. Why do we exist (what is our basic purpose)?
4. Who are our principal customers/clients/users? Are we primarily a production or a support operation?
5. What are our principal products/services/functions?
6. How do these products/services/functions contribute to the total organization's mission?
7. What is unique or distinctive about our unit's work as compared with other units in the organization?
8. What is different about our unit's business from what it was three to five years ago?
9. What is likely to be different about our unit's business three to five years in the future?
10. What is our unit's principal economic base (profit center, income generator, cost center, separate funding, part of larger profit or cost center, assigned budget, other)?
11. What should be our economic commitment to the total organization?
12. What philosophical issues are important to our organizational unit?
13. What special considerations do we have in regard to:
    - Upper management
    - Employees
    - Customers/clients/users
    - Suppliers
    - Peer organizations
    - General public
    - Others (specify)

---

depending on the interdependency and the practical limitations of conducting such sessions. At any rate, at some point each manager within the organization needs to know what the overall position of his or her particular unit is related to the total organization.

Figure 8.4 is a series of questions for clarifying organizational unit roles and missions. They are similar to those for the total organization (covered in the first book of this series) but are focused at the unit level.

How Should Unit Statements Be Prepared?

For an individual work unit, the following step-by-step process is recommended as a logical method by which a statement of roles and missions can be defined. Whether or not each step is followed precisely is a matter of choice, depending on local circumstances.

1. Identify the total organization's mission (either from its formal statement or by your own analysis).
2. Identify the roles and missions of the major department or functional unit of which you are a part.
3. Determine appropriate answers to the series of questions posed in Figure 8.4 that are relevant for you. (If possible, involve your key employees in this discussion and analysis.)
4. Prepare a rough draft of your roles and missions statement.
5. Check your draft statement against the key questions for evaluating unit roles and missions listed below. Force yourself to analyze the draft objectively. Invite others to assist you in the process.
6. Review this draft in depth with your immediate supervisor, your key direct employees, and any peer managers to whom it would be relevant. Modify it as appropriate.

Key Questions for Evaluating Unit Roles and Missions

The following questions should be uséd to validate or further modify a draft statement of unit roles and missions before final acceptance.

1. Does the statement include all *pertinent* commitments (for example, economic, functional, product, service, market, geographical)?
2. Is there a clear determination of production or support relationship?
3. Is the statement unique or distinctive in some way?

4. Is it consistent with, without duplicating, peer statements of roles and missions?
5. Is it understandable, brief, and concise?
6. Is the complete unit function stated and self-contained?
7. Does it provide a clear linkage to other, related roles and missions statements?

What Are Some Examples of Unit Roles and Missions?

The examples listed below are adapted from actual unit statements of roles and missions.

1. The mission of the Marketing Department is to contribute to the profitability and growth of the ABC Corporation through the effective marketing and sales of its present and future products and services. This will be carried out in the domestic industrial, educational, and governmental markets through direct sales and franchised dealers. This department exists in order to:
    *   Pinpoint and maintain contact with widely scattered, specialized markets throughout the United States
    *   Identify, qualify, and maintain contact with current and new influential buyers and decision makers in our markets
    *   Discover new uses and markets for existing products/ services and introduce new products/services effectively and economically
    *   Create a receptive audience for our products/services and our sales representatives
2. The mission of the Southwest Area Office is to carry out the mission of the agency in our assigned geographical area by:
    *   Continually assessing and responding to the related needs of the people and communities being served
    *   Effectively interpreting the agency's mission to those being served and to the general public
    *   Providing constructive feedback to the agency on local

acceptance of agency programs and the need for new
or modified services
- Ensuring cost-effective use of available resources
- Providing opportunities for meaningful and satisfy-
ing service and personal and career growth for all area
employees

3.   The mission of the Operations Department is to contrib-
ute to the profitability and growth of the ABC Commu-
nity Bank by providing high-quality bank operations
services to the bank's customers in the following areas:
- Teller services
- Bank-by-mail services
- Safe deposit services
- Contract collections
- New accounts
- Bookkeeping
- General ledger maintenance
- Monthly statements
- Cash maintenance and control
- Incoming and outgoing collections and transfers
- Clearings

This department exists in order to:
- Provide bank customers with rapid, accurate, and
courteous service designed to promote continuation
and expansion of a banking relationship
- Protect the interests of the bank through cost-effective
provision of services and by ensuring proper allocation of appropriate charges
- Promote and maintain a positive, helpful image for
the bank with its customers and the general public
- Create and maintain a mutually supportive working
and learning relationship among bank employees

In Summary

Although it is a strategic planning element, a statement
of unit roles and missions is an especially important document to be either developed or reviewed prior to starting the

unit operational planning process. That is why this supplement has been included, even though developing unit roles and missions is not actually a part of operational planning. This statement provides a foundation for clearly determining the efforts to be carried out at the unit level. Addressing the critical, ongoing expectations of the unit at least once a year provides greater assurance that the needs of the total organization will be met.

9

Making
Operational Planning
Work

Now that we have examined each of the elements and the various factors affecting them, it is time to bring them all together in a cohesive effort for operational plan development and implementation. Although each organization's specific requirements are unique to its own situation, there are some special considerations that can make operational planning work in your organization.

Operational plan *development* refers to the actual building or creation of the operational plan; it also includes the documentation of the plan. Operational plan *implementation* refers both to communication of the total plan throughout the organization, including the development of organizational unit plans, and actual execution of the plan.

Where Are You with Operational Planning?

Every organization has an operational plan of some sort, even if it is located primarily in the minds of one or more members of management. It may range anywhere from a complete operational plan to a budget to a sales plan to a "to do" list. The point is that you don't have to start over; you can begin wherever you are now in the planning process. In reviewing your current planning process, you need to answer three basic questions to determine what changes are needed:

- *Is your current planning process doing the job?* Does it clearly identify what needs to be accomplished for your organization to be successful? Does the plan lead to the kinds of effort that produce the results needed?
- *Is your current planning effort organization-wide in application?* Does it involve all managers and key employees in a planning effort that is integrated both vertically and horizontally?
- *How can your current planning process be strengthened?* What parts of the process, or of the organization, need attention to ensure greater consistency in your planning efforts?

The Planning Assessment Checklist, presented in Figure 9.1, is a tool that can both test the readiness of the organization for operational planning and quickly evaluate the effectiveness and completeness of current planning practices. It provides a quick overview of what is involved in operational planning, together with an opportunity for pinpointing specific additions or modifications that may be required. Actions to address these various deficiencies can then be initiated. The initial assessment normally is made by the CEO/COO, the senior executive team, and/or the planning process facilitator. Individuals who may be given assignments related to one or more of the factors on the checklist need to understand, and accept the responsibility for, whatever action may be expected.

Initially, whoever is making the assessment needs to go through the checklist, placing a check in the appropriate column for each item. *O.K.* means that the current planning process addresses that item satisfactorily. The process may need some fine tuning, but following existing practices is likely to produce the results desired. *Need* indicates either that the item should be added or that a more effective application is required than the one currently in use. After completing the initial checks, review each of the items that has a check in the *Need* column and determine what action is required, by when, and by whom. Figure 9.2 is an example of a checklist completed by a CEO. The checklist highlights those portions of the operational planning process that require special attention. It also provides a blueprint for getting started with the planning process.

What Is Involved in Implementing an Organization-Wide Approach?

In addition to what has already been covered regarding the implementation of an organization-wide approach to operational planning, there are some other special considerations to keep in mind.

- *A longer time span is required for organization-wide planning than for top-down planning.* This does not necessarily mean a greater investment of managerial time. It does mean that, because of the iterative nature of the process, more calendar time must be allocated to allow all relevant inputs to the process to be made. Depending on the size and complexity of the organization, operational planning, from initiation to final approval, is likely to take from two to four months of elapsed time, with three months a realistic average for a moderate-sized organization.
- *Managerial time investment should not be excessive,* assuming that most managers are already involved at least in budget preparation. While there will be many exceptions in either direction, executives and members of upper-middle management can expect to invest anywhere from four to seven total days of group effort over the time span of plan development. Normally, this will include a series of meetings, rather than a single, extended planning retreat, to allow for additional analysis that may be required as well as for the iterative process with organizational units. Lower-middle and first line managers

Figure 9.1. Planning Assessment Checklist.

Preplanning Factors	Current Status O.K.	Current Status Need	Action (When and by Whom)
Planning process model understood			
Planning roles clarified			
• CEO/COO			
• Senior executive team			
• Planning process facilitator			
Planning team selected			
Past planning results reviewed			
Plan to plan prepared			
Operational Planning			
Operational analysis completed			
• Issues identified and prioritized			
• Major conclusions reached			
Key results areas determined			
Indicators of performance identified			
Objectives selected (including standards of performance)			
Action plans prepared			
Budgets integrated			
Additional Considerations			
Cross-functional coordination			
Unit operational plans			
• Middle management			
• First line management			
Training/coaching			
Plan documentation			
Plan communication and understanding			
Plan review schedule			
Others			

Figure 9.2. Sample Completed Planning Assessment Checklist.

Planning Assessment Checklist

	Current Status		Action (When and by Whom)
Preplanning Factors	O.K.	Need	
Planning process model understood	✓		*update and reinforce*
Planning roles clarified			
• CEO/COO	✓		
• Senior executive team	✓		
• Planning process facilitator	✓		*Bill Scott*
Planning team selected	✓		
Past planning results reviewed		✓	*preplanning meeting 9/1 — me*
Plan to plan prepared		✓	*" 9/1 — Bill*
Operational Planning			
Operational analysis completed		✓	*Bill to prepare questionnaire for 9/1 meeting*
• Issues identified and prioritized		✓	
• Major conclusions reached		✓	*second meeting*
Key results areas determined	✓		
Indicators of performance identified		✓	*need to expand*
Objectives selected (including standards of performance)		✓	*need to tie in to indicators*
Action plans prepared	✓		
Budgets integrated		✓	*Jane to refine budget preparation process 9/15*
Additional Considerations			
Cross-functional coordination	✓		*need to reinforce*
Unit operational plans			
• Middle management	✓		
• First line management		✓	*Bill to coordinate training and implementation*
Training/coaching		✓	
Plan documentation	✓		
Plan communication and understanding		✓	*Bill to coordinate*
Plan review schedule		✓	*I will set ground rules 12/1*
Others			

probably will spend less time in operational plan development, because the nature of the plans tends to be more
clear-cut at those levels.

- *Planned information sharing, with appropriate feedback,
  should result in better communications.* Since the
  organization-wide planning approach is dependent on the
  sharing of information, both vertically and horizontally,
  better understanding of the plan and the planning process
  comes as a result. This requires a commitment, at all
  levels, to share plans with others with a need to know.
- *Less rework of plans and budgets should be required.* In
  many organizations, plans and budgets are submitted,
  revised, and resubmitted several times before they are
  finally accepted. Because of the information sharing that
  takes place in the organization-wide approach, and
  because the preparation of budgets is tied in so closely with
  the operational plan, less rework is normally required.
  Managers are better informed and therefore tend to do a
  more realistic and accurate job of plan preparation.
- *Developing and maintaining a planning schedule is
  critical.* Because of the number of pieces that need to come
  together, a realistic schedule must be established and
  adhered to. An effective tool for doing this is a *plan to
  plan.* This is not just a play on words. A plan to plan
  clearly identifies significant steps in the planning process
  that need to be completed if planning is to be an effective
  management tool. The plan to plan highlights the specific
  portions of the plan that need to be developed, sets a
  schedule for completion of each of these portions, and
  establishes a record of performance against that schedule.

Figure 9.3 is a sample plan to plan, including provision
for unit plan development. There are many variations on this,
of course, depending on the size of the organization and the
amount of unit plan development required. Each organization
needs to develop its own plan to plan, based on its specific
planning requirements. Typically, the final event in the plan
to plan will be review and approval by whoever has the final
say. Usually there is a specific time frame within which

Figure 9.3. Sample Plan to Plan.

Objective: To complete the operation plan for 19XX by December 1.

Action Steps	*Timetable*
1. Half-day preplanning meeting • Introduction to process • Review of prior plans • Identification of issues and operational analysis assignments	September 1
2. One-day planning meeting • Review of analysis assignments and agreement on issues and conclusions • Agreement on key results areas and indicators of performance	September 15
3. Dissemination of issues, conclusions, key results areas, and indicators of performance throughout organization for review and feedback	September 16–30
4. One-day planning meeting • Review and modification based on feedback • Agreement on preliminary objectives and action plans • Initiation of budget process	October 1
5. Preparation and submission of unit operational plans and budgets	October 2–30
6. One-day planning meeting • Review of unit plans and budgets • Agreement on alternatives to achieve objectives • Referral of unit plans for modification	November 1
7. Half-day planning meeting • Agreement on final objectives, action plans, and budgets	November 15
8. Documentation of operational plan	November 16–30
9. One-day planning meeting • Review of and final agreement on operational plan • Plan for implementation and monthly/ quarterly reviews	December 1

---

approval must take place. Approval may be by a board of directors, a parent company, a legislative body, or the CEO and the planning team themselves. By establishing a specific deadline by which approval must be obtained, it is possible to work backward and determine a realistic schedule for completion of each of the operational plan elements as well as for submission of unit plans.

What Does an Operational Plan Look Like?

One of the problems that frequently occurs in the preparation of an operational plan is the feeling that every detail must be included in the final document. Providing this amount of detail can be time-consuming, expensive, and in many ways counterproductive. For a moderate-sized organization, an annual operational plan normally will contain between fifteen and twenty-five pages. (See Figure 9.4 for a sample table of contents for an operational plan.) Information that is included in the organizational plan reflects only what will impact the total organization. Specific departmental or unit plans may be retained at a central location for reference purposes. However, including them in the total organizational plan tends to dilute its impact or invite unnecessary scrutiny of unit efforts. The total organization's operational plan should be a living document that is familiar to all key people within the organization and is reviewed formally on a regular basis. This cannot and will not be done with a large volume of material. Remember Morrisey's Law: the utility of any document is in inverse relationship to its length.

Once the operational plan for the total organization has been documented and approved, it is important that all key people throughout the organization be made aware of its contents and importance. While it will not necessarily be appropriate to distribute the entire plan throughout the organization, it is usually desirable to make an executive overview, which summarizes the key elements of the plan, available to everyone with a need to know. Specific portions of the plan may also be discussed at some length in meetings of departments or units that have implementation responsibility for those portions.

Figure 9.4. Sample Table of Contents for an Operational Plan.

	Pages
1. Executive Overview	1–2
2. Operational Analysis: Issues and Conclusions	3–6
• Focus on Current Product Threats	
• Maintain Profitability	
• Improve Customer Focus	
3. Key Results Areas and Indicators of Performance	7–8
• Description and Rationale	
4. Annual Objectives (Including Standards of Performance)	9
5. Action Plans	10–15
• Profitability	
• Sales Growth	
• New Product Development	
• Quality	
• Customer Service	
• People Development	
6. Budget Summaries	16–19
• Revenue	
• Expense	
• Capital	
• Cash Flow	
7. Plan Implementation and Review Schedule	20

When May Strategic and Operational Planning Be Completed Together?

As has been pointed out several times in this book, organizational planning is generally much more effective when strategic and operational planning are separated. However, in certain situations it may be either necessary or desirable to approach them simultaneously. For example:

• If an organization is embarking on a formal planning process for the first time, it may not be feasible to complete both the strategic and operational plans as distinctly separate efforts at different times. Recognizing that much of the initial effort may be placed in the operational plan in such a situation, it may be appropriate to address such things as organization mission and strategy as a preliminary effort to determining appropriate results for the coming year. The identification of critical issues, which can be incorporated as an early step, may address factors that have both strategic and operational significance. This simultaneous planning should be perceived as a temporary aberration that needs to be adjusted when a normal planning cycle can be instituted.

- A major unexpected event that will cause a significant change in direction for the organization may require substantial modification of the strategic plan while operational plans are being developed to meet short-term needs. For example, such things as technological break-throughs, unexpected new competition, restrictive legislation, or major crises (such as wars, boycotts, or critical shortages) may require an immediate modification of the organization's concept and direction. This modification may be a temporary adjustment or a complete and permanent change.

When circumstances suggest that both strategic and operational planning be addressed at the same time, the planning process facilitator needs to make certain that discussion of strategic issues is not overly cluttered with operational concerns. Even if the planning effort must be completed in a concentrated series of meetings, strategic elements, such as organization mission and strategy, should be formulated before specific objectives are determined.

What Is Different About Planning in Public Sector Organizations?

As has been evident throughout this book, the principles and practices of operational planning are equally applicable to governmental organizations as to companies in the private sector. The differences between the two kinds of organizations are far more in degree than they are in kind. Some of these differences, however, may need special attention. For example:

1. The budget cycle in governmental organizations tends to have significantly greater lead time than in most companies in the private sector. This means that the operational planning may have to be completed several months before what might be an ideal time. It may mean that greater consideration must be given to contingency plans in the event certain assumptions turn out to be invalid. For example, an unanticipated change in the economy could significantly alter the demand for welfare assistance from what was projected when plans were prepared.

2. The legislative process, and the political ramifications associated with that, is likely to influence the way plans are prepared and submitted for approval. For example, certain objectives an agency might wish to set that have strong political overtones could receive greater or lesser support during an election year than might be true during a nonelection year.

3. The media tend to have considerably more interest in reviewing and analyzing plans prepared by governmental agencies than those prepared by private corporations. So-called investigative reporters frequently look for proposed efforts that have "headline potential." Since in most cases governmental agency plans are in the public domain, some organizations may want to temper language and avoid certain details which, if taken out of context, could be interpreted as worthy of this year's "golden fleece" award.

4. Jurisdictional disputes over which agency should have responsibility for a particular effort may become particularly sensitive because of political overtones. A clear statement of mission (from a strategic plan) that is approved by the appropriate legislative body should at least reduce the potential of such jurisdictional disputes.

What Is the Difference Between an Operational Plan and a Business Plan?

There is a distinction between an operational plan and what is sometimes called a "business plan." A business plan, as referred to in financial circles, normally is prepared primarily for use in acquiring financing from venture capitalists or financial institutions and/or keeping them informed of detailed progress. Consequently, the business plan may require considerably more financial detail than is appropriate in the operational plan, which has as its primary purpose to provide guidance and direction for the rest of the organization. While the operational plan and the business plan are clearly related, each serves a distinctly different purpose. One should not be compromised in order to meet the needs of the other. (See the Annotated Bibliography for references on preparing a business plan.)

What About Management by Objectives?

Management by Objectives—or, as we refer to it, Management by Objectives and Results (MOR)—is primarily directed at individual managerial efforts rather than those of the total organization. The two processes are very clearly related, but they are not designed to accomplish the same purpose. MOR can be used to draw a distinction between an individual manager's projected accomplishments and those of that manager's organization. The manager who says, "My organization's objectives are my objectives," is only partially correct. Although a manager is held accountable for the results that are to be produced within his or her organizational unit, there are certain key results areas, such as people development, organizational relationships, and managerial responsibilities, that need to be separated from the unit plan. MOR is a powerful motivational tool for individual managers that is totally compatible with the approach to operational planning described in this book. It is also useful as a basis for performance appraisal. (For further information on the use of MOR, please refer to George Morrisey's texts, described in the Annotated Bibliography.)

What About Follow-Up?

A plan is only as good as its system for following up and ensuring performance designed to carry out the plan. Furthermore, since even the best-designed plans are based on assumptions and projections that may turn out to be inaccurate, provision must be made for modification of those plans in line with changing circumstances. New priorities or opportunities that may arise, a radical change in the marketplace, unexpected loss of available resources, and other such critical factors must be taken into consideration during the plan year. This is why regularly scheduled progress reviews related to plans must be conducted at least once a quarter, if not more frequently. Without a meaningful follow-up and control system, the planning process could end up being an exercise in futility.

In Summary

The development and implementation of an operational plan is the middle component in the Integrated Planning Process (see Figure 9.5). The operational plan clearly defines what the organization intends to accomplish during the coming year, and when and how this will take place. In addition, it is the means by which the current year of the organization's strategic plan is implemented. This requires the active involvement of the CEO/COO and the senior executive team, as well as all managers and key employees, in the operational planning process. The operational plan framework incorporates the six elements shown in Figure 9.6.

The three components of the Integrated Planning Process cover different aspects of planning and, therefore, are addressed initially at different times. The variables among the three are shown in Figure 9.7.

The strategic plan, as covered in the first book of this series, is visionary and long-range. The operational plan, addressed in this second book of the series, is specific and

Figure 9.5. Integrated Planning Process.

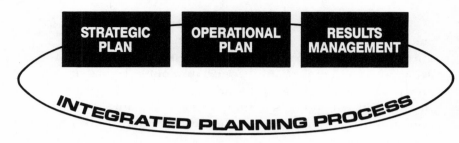

Figure 9.6. Operational Plan Framework.

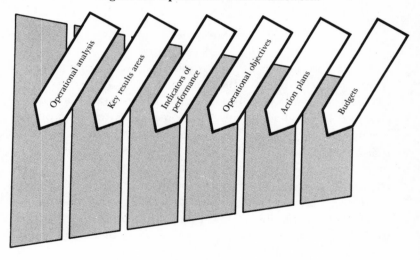

Figure 9.7. Key Variables in the Integrated Planning Process.

Components	Purpose	Emphasis	Level	Timing	Time Span
Strategic Plan	Concept Direction	External Broad	CEO Executive	Early in fiscal year	3–5 years
Operational Plan	Planned Results Resources	Internal Specific	CEO/COO All managers	Later in fiscal year	1 year
Results Management	Plan Execution Performance	Meaningful Reports Corrective Action	All managers Key employees	Daily Weekly Monthly Quarterly	Ongoing

short-term. Results management, the subject of the third book, closes the loop and is continuous in nature. All three must be integrated to ensure an effective, results-producing planning process.

The key to success in the Integrated Planning Process lies in getting the active involvement and commitment of everyone in the organization. Remember, the purpose of planning is not to produce plans; it is to produce results, and this requires total organizational commitment.

Annotated Bibliography

Below are listed a few selected books that provide additional insight into certain aspects of operational planning. We have annotated them to show their relevance.

General Management

Drucker, Peter F. *Management: Tasks, Responsibilities, Practices*. New York: Harper & Row, 1974.
    This book, from the man who has influenced modern management literature more than any other, continues to be a powerful guide for managers. It places planning in perspective as a unifying thread that can address all concerns as they arise. It is a *must* reference for any serious manager.

Geneen, Harold (with Alvin Moscow). *Managing*. New York: Doubleday, 1984.
    One of the most controversial corporate executives in U.S. corporate history, Harold Geneen provides tremendous insight into management and planning from a large-corporation perspective. While heavy-handed in implementation, Geneen's concepts are sound. They are summed up in the title of one of his chapters, "Managers Must Manage."

Grove, Andrew S. *High Output Management*. New York: Random House, 1983.

   Management as a team process, with particular emphasis on middle management, is the theme of this illuminating book by the president of Intel. His emphasis on the importance of integration in planning, as well as in other aspects of management, makes this worthwhile reading, particularly for managers in rapidly changing industries.

Iacocca, Lee (with William Novak). *Iacocca: An Autobiography*. New York: Bantam, 1984.

   In addition to being a fascinating story, this best-selling book is one of the most forthright and practical treatises on effective executive and managerial planning on the market today. Every manager—and would-be manager—should read it.

Kilmann, Ralph H. *Beyond the Quick Fix: Managing Five Tracks to Organizational Success*. San Francisco: Jossey-Bass, 1984.

   The author clearly establishes the premise that ongoing performance in today's rapidly changing business environment requires an integrated approach that does not rely on short-term fad solutions. His five tracks to organizational success fit right in with an integrated approach to planning.

Planning

Allen, Louis A. *Making Managerial Planning More Effective*. New York: McGraw-Hill, 1982.

   Louis Allen is one of the most respected seminal thinkers and writers in the field of management. This book provides a comprehensive coverage of planning from the perspective of the individual manager rather than of the enterprise as a whole. Chapter 8, "The Position Plan," is especially helpful for managers who need to define their own accountabilities as part of the total planning effort.

Below, Patrick J., George L. Morrisey, and Betty L. Acomb. *The Executive Guide to Strategic Planning.* San Francisco: Jossey-Bass, 1987.

The first in a three-book series on the Integrated Planning Process, this volume clearly defines how to approach and develop a strategic plan from the executive perspective. It shows the executive planning team how to put together a strategic plan in a way that provides clear direction to the rest of the organization in the preparation of supporting operational plans.

McConkey, Dale D. *Management by Objectives for Staff Managers.* Chicago: Vantage Press, 1972.

This book addresses itself specifically to the role of a staff manager and the particularly ambiguous status that role entails. The book faces head-on the traditional conflict problems and provides both a rationale and the tools for making the staff manager as much a part of the mainstream of operational planning as is any other manager.

Morrisey, George L. *Management by Objectives and Results for Business and Industry* (1977) and *Management by Objectives and Results in the Public Sector* (1976). Reading, Mass.: Addison-Wesley.

These two books address the process of operational planning primarily from an individual managerial perspective. Using the MOR approach outlined in these books, any manager at any level can develop a workable plan to accomplish that for which he or she is held accountable. While the process is the same in both books, the public sector version takes into consideration the special circumstances that a manager in government has to face.

Odiorne, George S. *MBO II: A System of Managerial Leadership for the 80s.* Belmont, Calif.: Fearon Pitman, 1979.

This is classic Odiorne in that it takes a systems approach to MBO, which ensures that it will outlast the fleeting life of a management label. MBO is presented as a planning system that interfaces with such subsystems as managerial selection, salary administration, zero-base budgeting, discipline, and the annual performance review.

Budgeting

Fleming, Mary M. K. *Managerial Accounting and Control Techniques for the Non-Accountant.* New York: Van Nostrand Reinhold, 1984.

This excellent book written for nonfinancial managers provides a clear outline of the differences between financial and managerial accounting. Longer and a bit more scholarly than the Ramsey book (below), it gets into several accounting areas, in addition to budgeting, that are important to managerial effectiveness. These include such things as pricing, managing inventories, and behavioral aspects of managerial accounting.

Pyhrr, Peter A. *Zero-Base Budgeting.* New York: Wiley, 1973.

The label "zero-base budgeting" does not inspire the same fervor that it did in the mid-1970s, but the conceptual impact of the approach in operational planning is still sound if we avoid some of the paperwork problems associated with it. This book was the first major work on the subject. It establishes clearly that budgets need to be justified in terms of what is to be accomplished each year rather than historical precedent. It provides a sound basis for making tradeoff decisions when budgeting cuts are required.

Ramsey, Jackson E., and Inez L. *Budgeting Basics: How to Survive the Budgeting Crisis.* New York: Franklin Watts, 1985.

This book is a gem. It takes a potentially dry subject, budgeting, and puts it into clear, easy-to-read, nonfinancial terms. The authors use a continuing case study throughout that is fun to follow. The chapter "New Department Budgeting" is especially helpful; it provides a good start-to-finish method, including how to make estimates on work-load, human resource skills, materials, and operating costs. The book provides everything a nonfinancial manager needs to know, and then some, about what goes into the preparation of budgets.

Business Plans

Hosmer, LaRue, and Roger Guiles. *Creating the Successful Business Plan for New Ventures.* New York: McGraw-Hill, 1985.

This is a powerful book for use by entrepreneurs in the development of small and medium-sized companies with up to $30 million annual sales. It takes the reader step by step through all the aspects of creating a business plan, with plenty of illustrations. It includes a completed business plan for an actual company.

Mancuso, Joseph R. *How to Write a Winning Business Plan.* Englewood Cliffs, N.J.: Prentice-Hall, 1985.

This highly readable book gets into such areas as how to "romance the money men" and how to locate hidden sources of capital, as well as what to put in an effective business plan. It includes the actual business plans for three successful companies.